"As I devoured this encouraging devotional, I saw the intentional hand of God woven throughout history by His precious daughters being used for His glory."

"*The Impact of Ordinary People* details the lives of obscure Bible characters with a significant impact on biblical history. These inspiring stories of women—viewed from a modern twist—will encourage you to keep reading. Don't miss it!"

—**ANNA RAMOS, PHD**,
LICENSED MENTAL HEALTH COUNSELOR (LMHC)

"*'Some of our women amazed us,'* exclaimed a Jesus follower to a stranger on the road to Emmaus (Luke 24:22, NIV). This was spoken before his spiritual eyes were opened to see the Lord. Don Wilkerson has opened our eyes to see and hear amazing voices of lesser-known women of the Bible. Many of them you will meet for the first time, learning the ways of God and how He has been speaking through women since the beginning of time. Read, learn, and enjoy this book."

—**KAY ZELLO**,
BIBLE TEACHER, CONFERENCE SPEAKER

"I was fascinated as I read through the stories of these lesser-known women in the Bible. Rizpah, Huldah, and Vashti are my favorite enlightening examples. As I devoured this encouraging devotional, I saw the intentional hand of God woven throughout history by His precious daughters being used for His glory. I was especially delighted to see Jael featured in this book! Our daughter's middle name is Jael, as we love the story of Jael's great courage. If you are a treasure seeker, then you'll want to discover the other hidden gems of women like Jael in the Bible. But don't take the word of this ordinary woman; read it for yourself and be built up in your faith today."

—**MARIAH NOELLE FREEMAN**,
AUTHOR, *FROM HEROIN TO HEAVEN*

The Impact of Ordinary People

30 DEVOTIONAL LESSONS FROM THE
LESSER-KNOWN **WOMEN** OF THE BIBLE

The Impact of Ordinary People

30 DEVOTIONAL LESSONS FROM THE
LESSER-KNOWN **WOMEN** OF THE BIBLE

Don Wilkerson

Newberry, FL 32669

Bridge-Logos
Newberry, FL 32669

The Impact of Ordinary People: 30 Devotional Lessons From the Lesser-Known Women of the Bible
by Don Wilkerson

Copyright © 2022 Bridge-Logos

All rights reserved. Under International Copyright Law, no part of this publication may be reproduced, stored, or transmitted by any means—electronic, mechanical, photographic (photocopy), recording, or otherwise—without written permission from the publisher.

Printed in the United States of America

Library of Congress Catalog Card Number: 2022937660

International Standard Book Number: 978-1-61036-279-5

Edited by Lynn Copeland

Cover/Interior design by Kent Jensen | knail.com

Cover illustrations: Distant Shores Media/Sweet Publishing, CC BY-SA 3.0 <https://creativecommons.org/licenses/by-sa/3.0>, via Wikimedia Commons

Unless otherwise noted, Scripture quotations are from the New King James Version®. Copyright © 1982 by Thomas Nelson. Used by permission. All rights reserved.

Scripture quotations marked NIV are from the Holy Bible, New International Version®, NIV® Copyright ©1973, 1978, 1984, 2011 by Biblica, Inc.® Used by permission. All rights reserved worldwide.

Scripture quotations marked NLT are from the *Holy Bible*, New Living Translation, copyright © 1996, 2004, 2015 by Tyndale House Foundation. Used by permission of Tyndale House Publishers, Inc., Carol Stream, Illinois 60188. All rights reserved.

Scripture quotations marked CEV are from the Contemporary English Version®, copyright © 1995 American Bible Society. All rights reserved.

Scripture quotations marked ESV are from The ESV® Bible (The Holy Bible, English Standard Version®). ESV® Text Edition: 2016. Copyright © 2001 by Crossway, a publishing ministry of Good News Publishers. All rights reserved.

BP 08/2022

CONTENTS

Introduction ix

1. Adah | A Mother Who Encouraged Her Son's Creativity... 1
2. Deborah No. 2 | Busy as a Bee......................... 5
3. Bilhah | A Surrogate Wife and Mother 9
4. Shiphrah & Puah | The First Prolife Workers........... 13
5. Achsah | A Daughter Who Wanted More 16
6. Jael | She Nailed It 19
7. Rizpah | Her Act of Honor Saved Israel from Famine 22
8. Zeruiah | A Mother of Great Influence 26
9. Abishag | A Woman Who Could Not Be Used 29
10. Jehosheba | Preserver of a Royal Seed................. 33
11. Abijah | Raising a Good Son Despite a Wicked Husband... 36
12. Bithiah | A Good Name in a Strange Place 40
13. Huldah | A Woman Who Sparked a Revival 43
14. Vashti | A Woman Who Said No 46
15. Gomer | A Woman Who Became a Sermon 51
16. Tamar No. 1 | Grace Greater Than Our Sin 55
17. Three Marys | Women in the Service of the Lord 59
18. Salome | A Model Mother 63
19. Anna | Growing Old Gracefully 66
20. Joanna | A Woman of Substance 70
21. Dorcas | Raised to Life 74
22. Rhoda | She Left Peter Outside of the Gate 78
23. Damaris | A Seed of Faith 81
24. Phoebe | Pure and Radiant as the Moon............... 84
25. Priscilla | The Strong Silent Partner 87

26. Julia | Called to be a Saint 91
27. Chloe | Part of the Problem or the Solution 95
28. Euodia & Syntyche | Called to Unity 99
29. Eunice | A Godly Heritage 102
30. Apphia | Welcoming a Prodigal..................... 105

Conclusion 109
Notes 111

INTRODUCTION

Most readers and students of the Bible are familiar with headliner female characters such as Mary, the mother of Jesus; Mary and Martha, the sisters of Lazarus; Esther, who became queen; Hannah the mother of Samuel, Mary Magdalene, Rahab, and other well-known women of the Bible. But what about some of the other Marys in the New Testament, or the almost thirty names Paul mentions in Romans chapter 16, many of which are of relatively unknown women. It is time to bring these names and their stories to light.

Part of the inspiration in writing this second book of my three-part series *The Impact of Ordinary People* came when I read Romans chapter 16 and found myself speed reading over the numerous names Paul mentions. Then, during one of those rushed readings, the Holy Spirit stopped me as if to say, why would Paul devote an entire chapter to remembering those who contributed so much in various ways to his mission and ministry? If they were important enough for Paul to remember and to write about, then I should know and remember them too.

Some of these lesser-known women are overshadowed by either a husband or son, such as Eunice, the mother of Timothy, or Mary, the mother of John Mark. A few may be better known than others, but they are included for various reasons in context when their brief background is given.

Several key lesser-known women are often passed over by most Bible readers, such as Abishag, who nursed King David on his deathbed; Damaris, who converted to the faith when Paul preached on Mars Hill in Athens; Dorcas, the first to be resurrected from the dead by Peter; and the prophetess Huldah, who sparked a revival in the Old Testament. I was reminded that Joseph had married the daughter of a heathen priest and that a controversy in a house church resulted in some of Paul's writing about the cross.

These names provide deep digs of treasures found in the Word of God, much like the treasures an archeologist might uncover at sites buried deep in the ground. In some cases, these lesser-known women are in plain sight but passed over due to the more significant events they are associated with. Like an investigator, I have searched deeply into the Bible and discovered the significant impact of these women.

Hopefully, women and men will find inspiration from the impact these seemingly ordinary women have made through biblical history. All of them play a part in the unfolding of the Bible's story of God and His Son. Each chapter provides proof of the *impact of ordinary people* both in Bible days and today.

1

Adah

A MOTHER WHO ENCOURAGED HER SON'S CREATIVITY

BACKGROUND: Genesis 4:15–22

KEY VERSE: *"And Adah bore Jabal…His brother's name was Jubal. He was the father of all those who play the harp and flute."* (Genesis 4:20,21)

Suppose long before the invention of an aircraft, a young boy looked at a bird flying and said to his mother, "One day, I'm going to make my own bird that people can fly." Might the mother think her son was too imaginative unless it turned out he was Orville Wright?

Go back to the beginning of time in the home of a mother named Adah, the first woman mentioned in the Bible after Eve. Adah was the first wife of Lamech, who bore him two sons: Jabal and Jubal. Suppose she sees Jubal trying to build something never seen before, using the bark of a tree. Might the mother scold him for spending so much time on the contraption, suggesting he quit his fool-hearted project? But then, one day, a unique sound comes out of the stringed instrument he made. His mother instead marvels at how her son Jubal had discovered that a piece of wood could be shaped into something that makes sound and music. Scripture says Jubal was known as "the father of all those who play the harp and flute" (Genesis 4:21). The point is that a parent, a mother or father, can either encourage or stifle a child's creativity.

Lamech's second wife, Zillah, bore a son they named Tubal-Cain, who the Bible says became "an instructor of every craftsman in bronze and iron" (Genesis 4:22). Such amazing creativity in one household. Perhaps Tubal-Cain helped his half-brother Jubal with his musical inventions and vice versa.

It would be good to think that both the boys' mothers and their father, Lamech, encouraged such visionary ideas and the process of Jubal inventing musical instruments and Tubal-Cain his craftsmen work. However, because music and craft work would become so important to the development of humanity, especially music important in worship, the hand of God and the anointing of the Holy Spirit must have been at work in these young men.

Myron and Esther Augsburger writing about creativity in *How to be a Christ-Shaped Family* stated:

> No human being should ever say, "I'm not creative," for this is denying a very important element of being made in the image of God. One of the special things about us...is creativity—the ability to make and do things beyond mere functional purposes, things with meaning. It is important to help our children understand this by guiding them to use their imagination in making things.[1]

Parents can either be stumbling blocks to their children's dreams or be supporters and motivators to pursue them. One of the worst parenting mistakes I made was with my son Todd, a talented basketball player in his small-town high school. He went on to play on a small college team, but his teenage dream was to play in the NBA someday. Instead of allowing him to find out the unlikelihood of this happening, I stuck a needle in his balloon, discouraging him from his dream. My wife scolded me for doing this, and rightly so. When Todd decided to become an actor to do TV commercials, I let events take their course without discouraging him, and he had immediate success on one of his first auditions. That commercial ran for some years. My wife and I enjoyed seeing him in numerous commercials, including three much-touted Super Bowl ads.

The world has been rightly blessed by Adah's two sons, especially with respect to music. Martin Luther wrote, "Music is one of the fairest and most glorious gifts of God, and takes its place next to theology.... Kings, princes, and lords must support music. Music is a discipline; it is instructive; it makes people milder and gentler, more moral, and more reasonable."[2]

I don't believe Jubal can be fully appreciated as the father of music without considering the encouragement he gained from his mother.

APPLICATION

1. Regarding Adah's sons, Matthew Henry wrote, "When Jabal had set them in a way to be rich [by building a livestock business], Jubal put them in a way to be merry."[3]
2. As parents, we can either foster or deflate the dreams of our children.

REFLECTION

- God shows the importance of music by gifting Jubal so early on in the dawn of creation.
- The gospel is preached by music, perhaps on a level higher than the spoken and printed word.
- It's good always to be aware of the root from which great gifts flow: by the Holy Spirit through mothers and fathers to their children.

2

Deborah No. 2

BUSY AS A BEE

BACKGROUND: Genesis 24:58–61; 35:8

KEY VERSE: *"So they sent their sister Rebekah on her way, along with her nurse…"*
(Genesis 24:59, NIV)

She was a simple yet loyal servant handmaid to Isaac's wife, Rebekah. She bore the same name as the first judge and prophetess in Israel, who had a prominent role as a fearless leader. Because Deborah no. 1 has such a high profile, she does not belong in the biblical list of lesser-known women. But Deborah no. 2 does, as we will discover. Why she is included here takes connecting certain dots of Bible characters.

The story of this Deborah begins with a simple mention of her name when Abraham sends his servant Eliezer to find a wife for his son Isaac among his relatives. This remarkable providential search is recorded in Genesis chapter 24. Bible scholars see Eliezer's success in finding Isaac's bride-to-be as a type of the Holy Spirit who seeks out the lost to become the bride of Christ (Revelation 21:2). In this case, Abraham's servant found a young girl named Rebekah. Her family left it up to Rebekah whether she would return with Eliezer to marry Isaac, and she agreed. This part of Scripture is where Deborah no. 2 comes into the picture. Genesis 24:59 says that they sent "Rebekah on her way, along with her nurse." That nurse was not named until much later in the book of Genesis.

We hear no mention of the nurse until eleven chapters later, when her death is recorded. The fact that her death and burial are mentioned in Scripture is most unusual and it is why she appears here as a person of impact.

Deborah was an ordinary person during all the years of service to Rebekah and the family of Isaac. But she had to be someone significant to them because she was given a special burial, recorded in Genesis 35:8. This verse begins, "Now Deborah...." So, the very first mention of her name is after serving Rebekah for decades. The verse goes on to say, "Now Deborah, Rebekah's nurse, died and was buried under the oak outside Bethel. So it was named Allon Bakuth." The latter name means "oak of weeping." From this we can add, without using too much imagination, that other family members were paying their respects to such a faithful servant of the Lord in service to the wife of Isaac, weeping under the oak tree where she was buried.

In the *Illustrated Dictionary of the Bible*, it indicates that Deborah was with Jacob at Bethel and "there she died at the age of about 155 years."[4] I find it quite interesting that the name Deborah means "bee." Lockyer aptly writes: "Deborah's conduct throughout her long life fulfilled the expectation, or hope, expressed by her name. As a bee symbolizes constant activity, industrious diligence and care, the God of grace enabled Deborah to live her life as a devoted, quiet and faithful nurse."[5] It appears Deborah lived her whole life selflessly for Rebekah, Isaac, and the extended family.

APPLICATION

1. When the love for God and for those being served is brought into such service, it raises it to a level of unparalleled godliness.
2. The old adage applies to Deborah: "Only one life, twill soon be past. Only what's done for Christ will last."[6] (C. T. Studd)

REFLECTION

- It is important to bring the most common duties to a place that glorifies God.
- "In the time we have it is surely our duty to do all the good we can to all the people we can in all the ways we can."[7] (William Barclay)

- A good testimony does not happen by happenstance; it usually results from good parentage, love for God, and love for people.

3

Bilhah

A SURROGATE WIFE AND MOTHER

BACKGROUND: Genesis 30:1–8; 35:19–22

KEY VERSE: *"Now when Rachel saw that she bore Jacob no children…she said, 'Here is my maid Bilhah; go in to her, and she will bear a child on my knees, that I also may have children by her.'"* (Genesis 30:1–3)

Bilhah was just a servant. She had no rights in the household, but taking a closer look at her role in the unfolding history of the Bible, there are some surprising revelations. In tracing certain unknown people in the Bible, connecting the dots is necessary to know the impact of such an ordinary person. Like me, you may read the verses on Bilhah and pass over how significant this person was at the time. It almost requires a magnifying glass to uncover who Bilhah was to the family of Jacob and his beloved wife Rachel and their heirs.

As was the custom in that time, when a wife was childless, she would offer her husband a servant girl in the house to become a surrogate mother. Rachel's reference to Bilhah to "bear a child on my knees" meant the servant would give birth to a child, but Rachel would be the child's mother as if it had come out of her womb. She was legally entitled to this claim. We first witness this in Scripture when Abraham's wife, Sarah, was promised a child in her old age but could not wait for God's answer, and, like Rachel, she gave her servant to her husband. So, Hagar birthed a child through Abraham.

We don't need to wonder what tension and turmoil this custom had between the birth mother and the mother who claimed the child as her own. In the case of Sarah, on one occasion, when she saw Hagar's son "mocking" (Genesis 21:9, NIV) and making fun of Isaac, she requested that Abraham send them away. Based on the case between Sarah and Hagar, we can assume the relationship between Bilhah, the birth mother, and Rachel, who raised the child as her own, was difficult.

Bilhah bore Jacob two sons, Dan and Naphtali, who played a significant future role in Israel's birth as a nation. Samson was birthed from the lineage of Dan, and so Bilhah too was Samson's progenitor. And Naphtali gave birth to a tribe by that name. Whether Bilhah saw any of this significant family tree unfolding, we do not know. We also don't know how Dan and Naphtali treated their birth mother.

These questions need to be asked when delving into the lineage, even of a servant girl.

Another reason I include Bilhah among the lesser-known women of the Bible is what happened between her and Jacob's firstborn son, Reuben, by Leah. His bio is quite interesting. He committed incest with Bilhah. Genesis 35:22 accounts that it must have created a widespread scandal, for the Word says, "Israel heard about it." Reuben paid dearly for his sin of incest. He was deprived of his birthright, which was given to the sons of Joseph (1 Chronicles 5:1). Reuben, then, lost the privilege given to a firstborn son. Lockyer writes, "No judge, no prophet, no hero sprung from Reuben. By his sin Reuben had permanently impoverished his posterity."[8]

When the history of the Reubenites is compared with that of the Danites and the tribe of Naphtali, we find Bilhah has quite an ancestry. Today we hear how adopted children often search for their birth mother, and some inspiring stories come from the uniting of biological mother and child. Did Dan and Naphtali know the circumstances of their birth? Did they ever have a relationship with their birth mother, Bilhah? Regardless of these unanswered questions, there are spiritual lessons that can be applied.

APPLICATION

1. God employs many simple servants to do His will. It may not be the normal manner of childbirth as arranged by Rachel and Jacob with a servant girl, but once done the sons born from that union became a part of her spiritual and family legacy. These are God mysteries often unexplainable in the natural.
2. The grace of God can shine through despite sinful actions in a family.

REFLECTION

- We become children of God by faith (though all children, regardless of the circumstances of their birth, belong to God—even in the womb).
- In the Old Testament, a child birthed by a surrogate can be loved by both mothers, as is the beauty of adoption today.

4

Shiphrah & Puah

THE FIRST PROLIFE WORKERS

BACKGROUND: Exodus 1:8–22

KEY VERSE: *"So the king of Egypt called for the midwives and said to them, 'Why have you done this thing, and saved the male children alive?'"* (Exodus 1:18)

These two Hebrew women are unsung heroes in the history of the Israelites—they were instrumental in saving the lives of Hebrew boys, especially Moses. The role of midwives was to assist women during childbirth and care for their babies. Shiphrah and Puah were either singled out by Pharaoh because they were supervisors of other midwives or were known for their particular skills regarding childbirth. Whatever the reason, Pharaoh asked the wrong people to help kill Hebrew newborns.

These women feared God and refused Pharaoh's command. God rewarded their courage: "Therefore God dealt well with the midwives, and the people [of God] multiplied and grew very mighty. And so it was, because the midwives feared God, that He provided households for them" (Exodus 1:20,21).

Shiphrah and Puah represent the multitude of healthcare workers and midwives today who deliver babies, as well as the staff and volunteers in pregnancy resource centers who give counsel and help to expectant mothers as an alternative to abortion. Today countless women and men stand courageous to protect life, defying our culture that wants to normalize the death of babies through abortion.

A recent example of someone standing against abortion is a woman named Serena Dyksen. She has written a book with Julie Klose (my daughter) entitled *She Found His Grace*. The back cover of the book states: "At the age of thirteen, Serena Dyksen was raped, pregnant, and taken to an abortion clinic. Abortion was supposed to be the answer after Serena's trauma, but instead it tore her family apart and nearly destroyed her life. Terrible things happen behind the doors of the abortion clinic."[9]

Serena is now an outspoken prolife advocate against abortion. Today we can be grateful for the many prolife advocates who stand against morally wrong abortion "rights." Because of them, how many women are protected from going through the trauma of abortion that Serena experienced? How many babies are saved? All it takes is the courage to protect life, like the two Hebrew midwives who defied Pharaoh. The evangelical church needs to be stronger in a call to action against abortion in both the political and spiritual arenas.

APPLICATION

1. The Bible is very clear as to what God thinks about what takes place in a woman's womb. "You are the one who put me together inside my mother's body, and I praise you because of the wonderful way you created me. Everything you do is marvelous! Of this I have no doubt" (Psalm 139:13,14, CEV).
2. Thank God for ministries and organizations like Prolife Across America that put up billboard signs, from Times Square to rural America, showing images of newborn babes and advocating prolife.

REFLECTION

- Being prolife is not a political issue, it's a biblical one, and a matter of life or death.
- Attention should be given to the stories of those who survived an abortion. Their life is a living testimony to why the prolife message needs promotion.
- God will show grace to those who have had an abortion and confess it to God in repentance.

5

Achsah

A DAUGHTER WHO WANTED MORE

BACKGROUND: Joshua 15:13–19

KEY VERSE: *"Right after the wedding, Achsah started telling Othniel that he ought to ask her father for a field."* (Joshua 15:17,18, CEV)

Buried deep in the book of Joshua is the name of Caleb's newly married daughter, Achsah. From a brief encounter with her father, we learned that she was bold, ambitious, and probably had an entrepreneurial spirit. She typifies those who want more territory, more blessings, more for their future family, and more of God.

Achsah's story is as follows: her father challenged some of his warriors to capture a particular city, and whoever was responsible for doing so would win his daughter, Achsah, in marriage. The winner was Othniel, the nephew of Caleb. Keeping his promise, Caleb blessed the marriage of Othniel to Achsah.

Immediately after the wedding, Achsah asked her father for some springs of water, and "Caleb gave her a couple of small ponds, named Higher Pond and Lower Pond" (Joshua 15:19). This request may have been so the couple could develop an investment in livestock to make a living. The ponds were actually springs.

We also know the marriage might have been prosperous because Othniel later brought Israel back from idol worship and an eight-year captivity under a Syrian king and led God's people through a time of peace and prosperity (Judges 3:7–10).

Achsah stands out during the time of the Israelites' conquest of the Promised Land. Joshua may have included this in their history out of admiration for Caleb's daughter's boldness. In the culture of the time, women were to be seen and rarely heard. Achsah was brave and bold for what she was asking. Her husband might have thought it was not his place to ask for more territory, after all, he's already been awarded Caleb's daughter as his wife. That may be why Achsah asked instead.

I include Achsah in the lesser-known Bible characters because she is a type who spiritually desires more of God—springs of living water for a thirsty soul. For some, *more* might be motivated by a worldly desire. Those who seek things above are sometimes trusted with better things below because God can trust them to keep their priorities in order.

APPLICATION

1. One of the best prayers we can pray is "more, Lord." More of You. More lost souls saved! More going out into the field of harvest. "But I will hope continually, and will praise You yet more and more" (Psalm 71:14). "May the Lord give you increase more and more" (Psalm 115:14).
2. God is the giver of abundant life (John 10:10) and abundant resources (2 Corinthians 9:8), and He provides more than even was asked of Him (Ephesians 3:20).

REFLECTION

- There is a danger of wanting more when it's the wrong thing.
- "Abundance, like want, ruins many." (Romanian proverb)
- Be bold in asking God for things that are about advancing His kingdom on earth.

6

Jael

SHE NAILED IT!

BACKGROUND: Judges 4:12–24

KEY VERSE: *"Sisera was exhausted and soon fell fast asleep. Jael took a hammer and drove a tent-peg through his head into the ground, and he died."*
(Judges 4:21, CEV)

Jael's method of execution was treacherous but what she did was put the final nail in the coffin, so to speak, of Israel's enemy under King Jabin. "Jabin's army had nine hundred iron chariots, and for twenty years he made life miserable for the Israelites, until finally they begged the Lord for help" (Judges 4:1–3, CEV). Sisera was the commander of that army.

An army of ten thousand Israelites, led by Barak, went up against Sisera and his chariot-riding army and entirely wiped them out. But Sisera escaped. We have seen throughout Scripture that even one enemy could continue to be a threat to Israel. Sisera's escape could have been dangerous for Israel. But God had other plans for him.

He ran into the tent of Jael—a place he probably was familiar with because Jael's husband Heber had a peace agreement with King Jabin. So he flees to her tent thinking it a safe place to hide from Barak. God takes the foolish things of the world to confound the wise and mighty (see 1 Corinthians 1:27), and such was the case of what took place in Jael's tent. She pretends she will keep watch for Sisera's enemy but instead gives him warm milk to drink (possibly with herbs that help with sleeping). The milk then may have acted as a sedative for this exhausted army general. He fell asleep and never woke up as Jael took a tent peg and drove it into the temple of his head. And so this ordinary woman commits the final act of war, nailing down the victory for God's people in answer to their prayer.

Down through history God has selected the right man or, as in this story, the right woman to use whatever normal or abnormal means He chooses to accomplish His will. With God, one person can be a majority: "One man of you shall chase a thousand, for the LORD your God is He who fights for you, as He promised you" (Joshua 23:10).

Who would have thought that this woman—not a worshiper of Jehovah, not an Israelite—would become an instrument in the hand of God to assist in achieving a victory over Israel's enemies? God has at His disposal whatever is necessary to protect His people and defeat those persons or forces that seek to oppose the work of God. It may be a strange prayer to pray: Lord raise up a Jael to overcome evil and accomplish good for Your glory.

APPLICATION

1. Remember, God's mathematics is different than ours. He does better with three hundred than three thousand; He needs only five loaves and two fish to feed five thousand plus; and all He needed was a Jael to "nail" down a victory.
2. If we don't kill a persistent temptation, it can be the cause of our spiritual death. We need to let Christ take care of it through putting a nail in the thing that is alive in us.

REFLECTION

- Beware of the enemy disguising himself as an angel of light that knocks on your door. If he gets in, kick him out as soon as possible in the name of Jesus. He will knock again. Don't answer the door.
- It takes more than the milk of the Word to overcome some temptations; better to use the Sword of the Lord covered with anointing oil.
- Never underestimate the power of a woman when she stands up to the enemy.

7

Rizpah

HER ACT OF HONOR
SAVED ISRAEL FROM FAMINE

BACKGROUND: 2 Samuel 21:1–14

KEY VERSE: *"Rizpah...spread burlap on a rock and stayed there the entire harvest season."*
(2 Samuel 21:10, NLT)

In one of the most unusual stories in the Old Testament, a mother named Rizpah spent weeks watching over the dead bodies of two of her sons, plus five others (all descendants of King Saul), all of whom were hung on a mountain top. This grieving, determined mother "stayed there the entire harvest season. She prevented the scavenger birds from tearing at their bodies during the day and stopped wild animals from eating them at night" (2 Samuel 21:10, NLT).

This created a bizarre scene for those who would have witnessed it, and news spread. Now take into account that there was a three-year famine in the land, and King David prayed to the Lord about it, and He answered, "The famine has come because Saul and his family are guilty of murdering the Gibeonites" (2 Samuel 21:1, NLT). Saul had tried to kill all the Gibeonites while he was king.

The Gibeonites wanted to avenge what Saul did in trying to destroy them as a people. David asked, "What can I do then? Just tell me and I will do it for you" (2 Samuel 21:4, NLT). They asked for seven of Saul's sons, including grandsons, to be handed over to them. Rizpah's sons Armoni and Mephibosheth were handed over to the Gibeonites and killed along with five of Saul's grandsons.

Rizpah's act of dedication and honor was done so that her sons could have a decent burial. She spread burlap out and guarded all the men's bodies, including her sons'. This was apparently quite a spectacle seeing this ordinary woman doing such an extraordinary thing to seek honor for the dead men.

King David noticed what Rizpah was doing and realized he'd not given a proper burial for Saul and Jonathan. "So David obtained the bones of Saul and Jonathan, as well as the bones of the men the Gibeonites had executed. Then the king ordered that they bury the bones in the tomb of Kish, Saul's father..." (2 Samuel 21:13,14, NLT). Because of Rizpah's act of honor that led to the proper burial of Saul and his descendants, "God answered prayer in behalf of the land" (2 Samuel 21:14, NIV), and the famine ended.

One of the most neglected truths and teaching in the church, especially in the training of ministers, is the importance of giving honor to whom honor is due. When Noah got drunk and became uncovered in his tent, his youngest son laughed and made light of it. The older, more mature brothers took a sheet, walked backward, and covered their father's nakedness and shame (see Genesis 9:20–23). Might we need to say at times, "Pass the sheet." There are times honor is given when love covers a multitude of sins.

APPLICATION

1. "It's easy to honor someone you don't know. But to honor some you do know, after seeing the good, the bad, and ugly in their lives…this is the real challenge." (Source unknown)
2. I recommend John Bevere's book entitled *Honor's Reward*, a book I read in my sixties that I wished I'd been able to read in my twenties before I went into the ministry.

REFLECTION

- Honor given to those who did not earn it is a waste of words.

- You can't buy honor though many try. It is earned, and those who earn it rarely think they deserve it.
- "I would prefer to fail with honor than win by cheating." (Sophocles, a Greek playwright)

8

Zeruiah

A MOTHER OF GREAT INFLUENCE

BACKGROUND: 1 Kings 2:1–6

KEY VERSE: *"Moreover you also know what Joab the son of Zeruiah did to me...."* (1 Kings 2:5)

Mothers influence for better or for worse. I have watched certain celebrity athletes who convey humility, graciousness, and good character, and I say quietly to myself, "He must have had a good mother" or, "She probably was raised by a good mother." Children are often known by the influence of a good and godly mother.

We don't know much about Zeruiah, but a key reference is the fact that she was David's sister (1 Chronicles 2:13–16). She became known as a loyal sister, as she and her family are numbered among the community that fled with her brother David from Saul. Zeruiah seems to have influenced her brother, her family, and the community because she is mentioned several times when Israel's history is recounted.

She must have been known as a good and godly mother who influenced her children because when Scripture references her three sons, Abishai, Joab, and Asahel, it refers to them with respect to her as their mother (2 Samuel 2:18). King David referred to her name when mentioning her three sons: "And today, though I am the anointed king, I am weak, and these sons of Zeruiah are too strong for me" (2 Samuel 3:39, NIV). In fact, Zeruiah is mentioned more than any other mother in Scripture in regard to sons.

Good roots produce good fruit. Outstanding sons and daughters are most often the product of their upbringing. Of Zeruiah's three sons, David's nephews, we know Abishai was also one of David's thirty military leaders to whom he gave special mention at the end of his life. Joab was also a skilled military leader with David until he became overly ambitious, put himself first before David, and paid dearly for it after David's death. Godly influence does not last a lifetime, and children make their own decisions, some not so good. But mothers who "train up a child in the way he should go" (Proverbs 22:6) are instilling godly influence not only in their family but in the next generation.

APPLICATION

1. "A mother's heart [like Zeruiah's] is the child's schoolroom." (Henry Ward Beecher)
2. Zeruiah was the sister of David, so she began life with a good example and heritage. Honor the good examples God has placed in your life.

REFLECTION

- A Jewish proverb says, "God could not be everywhere, so He made mothers."
- I have seen parents' sins come out through their children, and I have also seen the righteous seeds planted in children bear much fruit, sometimes for generations to come.
- "God Himself appreciates the influence of a Christian mother in the molding of character in her children."[10]

9

Abishag

A WOMAN WHO COULD NOT BE USED

BACKGROUND: 1 Kings 2:10–25

KEY VERSE: *"Now I ask one petition of you; do not deny me. And she [Bathsheba] said to him, 'Say it.' Then he said, 'Please speak to King Solomon, for he will not refuse you, that he may give me Abishag the Shunammite as wife.'"* (1 Kings 2:16,17)

Abishag was chosen to be a nurse and caregiver for David in his elder years. Although she was considered a part of the king's harem, her assignment was by modern standards quite different, for she was to sleep with David to warm his body, but she was not to be "known" by him in a sexual manner (see 1 Kings 1:4). This was just a practical matter in those times, but she may have come too late, as David died not long after Abishag took on this assignment.

We can assume she remained as part of the king's harem since Adonijah, David's fourth son, asks Bathsheba to intervene for him in requesting that Solomon give him Abishag as his wife. She was chosen as David's nurse because she was a virgin and because of her beauty, youth, and vitality. Adonijah was aware of her when she began caring for his father, David.

Adonijah was handsome with great charisma. Before Solomon was declared the future king by his father, David, Adonijah aspired to the throne. When David was dying, Adonijah called a meeting of the sons of David, his brothers, and the men of Judah—all except Solomon. This was to proclaim himself king. Nathan got wind of it and informed Bathsheba, urging that they both go to David (1:1–14). David then gave orders to Zadok, Nathan, and Benaiah to publicly anoint Solomon king and set him on David's throne (1:32–35). Apparently, since Adonijah couldn't seize the throne, he wanted the woman who was at the center of David's life at the time. After this, Solomon had every reason to question Adonijah's loyalty.

Therefore, when Bathsheba brought the marriage request to Solomon, he did not take it well. Perhaps Bathsheba may have thought this marriage would appease Adonijah from pursuing his father's throne in the future. Solomon, however, smelled a plot, one that sought to use the young girl for a devious motive. Although David had not slept with

Abishag, she would still have been considered a part of his harem. Had Solomon died, Adonijah would have inherited the throne through her. Therefore, when the proposition was brought to Solomon, he reacted sternly.

This was the story behind Solomon refusing to heed his mother's request in Adonijah's effort to marry the young virgin from Shunem. That request resulted in Adonijah's death, ordered by Solomon.

In all this, Abishag was an innocent party. Whether she even knew Adonijah's history, we don't know. But we do know enough in this saga to point out some lessons and spiritual applications.

APPLICATION

1. Men have often used women for devious means. I've seen a pastor's wife or children used, like Adonijah used Bathsheba, to appeal to the pastor for specific requests. The request might be innocent or unethical. Of course, a woman can use a man for the same reason.
2. Manipulation comes in many forms, and we need to be always discerning of its possibility. Discernment of other intentions is necessary at times. Be alert when others may be drawing you into what looks good but, in the end, may not be a good decision or action.

REFLECTION

- "There is a path before each person that seems right, but it ends in death" (Proverbs 16:25, NLT).
- It can be embarrassing to find out you are being used or manipulated. Better late than never. Good intentions can become the wrong intentions if you find out there is a scheme going on.
- Mothers especially, such as in this case, are vulnerable to manipulation in advancing a child's quest for something or someone. James and John requested their mother ask Jesus for an important position in what they thought would be His kingdom on earth (Matthew 20:20–22).

10

Jehosheba

PRESERVER OF A ROYAL SEED

BACKGROUND: 2 Kings 9:14–29; 11:1–3

KEY VERSE: *"But Ahaziah's sister Jehosheba...took Ahaziah's infant son, Joash, and stole him away from among the rest of the king's children, who were about to be killed."* (2 Kings 11:2, NLT)

Jehosheba undertook this courageous act of saving her nephew because when her brother Ahaziah, king of Judah, had been killed, his mother Athaliah began to destroy the rest of the royal family—her grandsons. She then reigned as queen as the only woman to do so in Judah.

Miraculously, when the murderous mother was doing her dastardly deed, Jehosheba took ("stole") one of the heirs, a six-year-old boy named Joash, and saved him from being murdered. This was done right under the nose of those killing off the king's other sons. Even more remarkable was that she was the sister of Ahaziah, who was married to the daughter of Ahab and Jezebel. What a heritage Joash had to overcome.

Jehosheba was the wife of the high priest, which made it doubly risky for her when the official religion at the time was the worship of Baal. Read 2 Kings 11:4–12 about another godly and ordinary man of impact, in this case, a priest named Jehoiada. He and his wife kept the rightful heir to the throne hidden in the Temple for six years, providing around-the-clock security at the Temple to keep Joash safe. The security team was told to "kill anyone who tries to break through. Stay with the king wherever he goes" (2 Kings 11:8). Joash was already being called king though he was still a child.

When Joash was seven years old, they "placed the crown on his head, and presented him with a copy of God's law [probably more symbolic as he might have just begun to learn to read]. They anointed him and proclaimed him king and everyone clapped their hands and shouted, 'Long live the king!'" (2 Kings 11:12). How must Jehosheba have felt at such a moment?

Joash's forty-year reign as king did not end well, but the son of a wicked father, Ahaziah, ruled righteously for decades because he was nurtured by such a woman of God and her husband, a temple priest. Joash showed his weakness after Jehoiada died. He did not stand firm against ungodly leaders who reversed the reforms Joash had instituted under the influence of Jehoiada. Yet, none of this can take away from the heroic work of Jehosheba in preserving a righteous seed in a time of the slaughter of Joash's brothers.

APPLICATION

1. Behind the scenes, there are often women doing heroic deeds no one knows of until later.
2. Investment in the lives of children by parents and the church prepare them to be the King's kids who can grow up and serve the Lord.

REFLECTION

- Sometimes it's God's will to tear down idolatry in the Lord's house, as was done under the priestly authority of Jehoiada (2 Kings 11:14).
- Jehosheba means "Jehovah is her oath." We can take that to mean she had given herself to God, His work, and His will as a lifetime commitment.
- When Joash's mentor Jehoiada died, so did Joash spiritually. Leaders need godly mentors not just in their younger years but all through their lives. Pride ruins some leaders who think they reach a point where they no longer need accountability.

11

Abijah

RAISING A GOOD SON
DESPITE A WICKED HUSBAND

BACKGROUND: 2 Kings 18:1–6

KEY VERSE: *"[Hezekiah] was twenty-five years old when he became king, and he reigned in Jerusalem twenty-nine years. His mother's name was Abijah daughter of Zechariah."* (2 Kings 18:2, NIV)

In my years working with those needing recovery and transformation for a life-controlling problem, I witnessed how some individuals came from broken homes. There are two kinds of broken homes. One is when husband and wife are divorced or separated, and another type of separation is when one person starts following the Lord while the other does not.

Abijah came from a marriage separated by faith and commitment to God. Her name means "Jehovah is God," as well as "the will of God." We take from this that she was true to her name and clung to the fatherhood of God, seeking to do His will. Thus, the logical conclusion is that this godly mother raised Hezekiah, and he went on to rule according to God's ways inherited from his mother and not from his father, Ahaz.

Ahaz served as king between two good men, Jotham, his father, and Hezekiah, his son. It is not that Ahaz did not know the truth of Jehovah God. It was demonstrated by Abijah's example of godliness that must have existed in his marriage to her. Because the Scripture says Abijah was the daughter of Zechariah, it is further evidence of her faithfulness to the Lord. Zechariah, it says, "had understanding in the visions of God" (2 Chronicles 26:5) and thus must have influenced the household of Abijah, where Hezekiah was raised.

Ahaz was given a clear witness by the prophet Isaiah. The first amazing prophecy of the future birth of Israel's Savior was given to Ahaz. Lockyer writes concerning this: "Let it not be forgotten that it was to king Ahaz that Isaiah's first evangelistic announcement was made in the promise of Emmanuel. The prophet sent a message to terrified Ahaz, but he would not turn to God and trust His deliverance. In order to help restore the faith of the wavering king, Isaiah urged Ahaz to ask for a sign from Jehovah, but he refused and in rejecting the message of hope, forfeited his soul."[11]

I cannot help but wonder if his wife, Abijah, urged him to do the right thing and prayed for her husband to turn to God. If so, Hezekiah may have been an eyewitness to Isaiah's call of repentance to his father. Ahaz could have and should have shown the strength of a righteous leader at a time when the nation was corrupted by "a brood of evildoers," and religion had become just a ritual (Isaiah 1:4,13).

It was not until Hezekiah reigned as his father's successor and kept the Lord's commands that "the LORD was with him; he prospered wherever he went" (2 Kings 18:7). All this can, in some part, be traced back to his godly mother.

APPLICATION

1. God always has a witness even in times of apostasy. The message of hope to Ahaz was clear from the prophet of God. He chose not to lead his people the right way but gave in to their sins. In this respect, history is continuously repeated. As Matthew Henry stated, "Apostasy is worse than the state of ignorance."[12]
2. Proverbs 22:6 promises that if a child is trained up in the ways of God, he will continue to follow the right way when he grows up. The story of Abijah and Hezekiah is an example of this Bible promise.

REFLECTION

- A mother's influence can change a society. Her son, Hezekiah, undid all of his father's evil leadership. His godly influences spread like an aroma throughout the land. These words and

phrases describe his rule: prosper, obedient, held fast to the Lord, and subdued enemies of the land.
- Sometimes a good mother must protect her children from bad influences coming against them. We can only imagine what Abijah had to do to protect Hezekiah from the evil influence of her husband.

12

Bithiah

A GOOD NAME IN A STRANGE PLACE

BACKGROUND: 1 Chronicles 4:17,18

KEY VERSE: *"And these were the sons of Bithiah the daughter of Pharaoh, whom Mered took."* (1 Chronicles 4:18)

My discovery of Bithiah may be one of the most surprising and even amazing among all the lesser-known women in this gallery of Bible characters. Bithiah's father was a Pharaoh and she was married to an Israelite. As the Scripture says, Mered took her as his wife. Therein is a mystery.

Mered was the son of Ezrah, a descendant of Judah through Caleb, Joshua's assistant. Where then did Bithiah and Mered meet and subsequently get married? Was it in Egypt? Unlikely! We must assume Bithiah became an Israelite proselyte. This is the remarkable part of this story. When the Jews came out of Egypt toward the Promised Land, the Bible says that "a mixed multitude went up with them" of those who left Egypt upon their liberation (Exodus 12:38). We can assume they were culturally and religiously mixed.

Bithiah is a Hebrew name, and it is unlikely this was her birth name but rather an adopted name when she embraced the Hebrew religion. Her name means "daughter of Jehovah." The question is, when and how did she become a Hebrew convert? At what age? By what influence? She and Moses grew up in the same household; so what was their age difference? Like all Egyptians, she most likely witnessed the ten plagues in Egypt. For example, could she have noticed the children of Israel had light in their dwellings while the rest of Egypt was in darkness for three days (Exodus 10:22,23)? Is it possible that by this ninth plague, Pharaoh's daughter had already decided to leave Egypt?

Most of what I write about this daughter of Pharaoh, particularly about her conversion, we can consider circumstantial evidence. However, the critical evidence is her marriage to Mered, who clearly was an Israelite.

APPLICATION

1. Bithiah is one of the incredible miracles hidden in plain sight in the Scriptures and a preview of the power of the gospel to reach someone steeped in an ungodly household and heathen land, even that of the Pharaoh.

2. That Bithiah embraced the God of the Israelites should not be surprising in that another of Pharaoh's daughters saved Moses from drowning, enabling God to use him to save his people from bondage.

REFLECTION

- From the very beginning, God has taken nothing and made something out of it. As in physical creation, so is a spiritual new creation (2 Corinthians 5:17).
- The name Bithiah means "daughter of Jehovah." It's just like the Lord to take a daughter of Pharaoh and transform her into a *daughter of Jehovah*.

13

Huldah

A WOMAN WHO SPARKED A REVIVAL

BACKGROUND: 2 Chronicles 34:14–33

KEY VERSE: *"So Hilkiah and those the king had appointed went to Huldah the prophetess…And they spoke to her to that effect…Then the king stood in his place and made a covenant before the LORD, to follow the LORD, and to keep His commandments…"*
(2 Chronicles 34:22,31)

Huldah was a prophetess in the Old Testament with a reputation like that of Deborah and Hannah. Her husband was the keeper of the royal wardrobe for the temple. As a prophetess during the reign of Josiah, Huldah would probably have had a seat of honor in the town square where she made herself available for all who had questions about Jehovah.

The people learned about Jehovah this way, until one day a priest found a scroll in the temple containing the writings of Moses, which we now call the Pentateuch. It was gathering dust, and no one was reading it or passing on the law to the people so it could be obeyed. So Huldah was called to authenticate that this was the Word of God, and she confirmed it, including the warning that unless the revelation of Moses' truth were followed, there would be doom and judgment in the land.

Huldah's prophecy gave King Josiah greater courage to put into practice the laws that were written. He acted swiftly bringing together the priests and prophets and every class of people in the land. The king stood before the throng and began reading aloud Moses's writing, also called the Covenant of Commitment, which might be called a consecration service in later times in the church. On behalf of the people, Josiah repented and said he would follow the Word of God fully and had everyone listening pledge to do the same.

From that day forward, there was a national revival with everyone starting fresh in doing what needed to be done according to God's Word. There was a national cleansing of the spiritual pollution in the land. Holiness and righteous living were reestablished, and all through Josiah's reign he shepherded the people making sure they kept their commitment.

It all started when one prophetess with a godly reputation told the people what the Lord said to her and thereby helped the king to institute the law as a part of the Temple worship and the practices in the people's way of life. It was one of the most remarkable revivals in Old Testament times.

APPLICATION

1. Whenever a people, a church, or even a nation enacts the truth of God's Word into their personal lives and practices, a spiritual and moral revival will occur.
2. Ministers, leaders, and shepherds need to lead the way in preaching prophetic truths based on God's Word and not on a misinterpretation of fundamental truths.

REFLECTION

- Sometimes revival happens when one person rises to speak a prophetic word.
- Revival is not for show. It begins best through quiet repentance, humility, and brokenness. The shouting can come later.
- What would happen if a revival of the Word through preaching, daily family reading of the Bible, and other public events centered on reading Scripture rather than just praise and worship? Word first! Worship second.

14

Vashti

A WOMAN WHO SAID NO

BACKGROUND: Esther 1:5–2:1

KEY VERSE: *"But Queen Vashti refused to come at the king's command..."* (Esther 1:12)

Although a queen is not considered an ordinary person, I include Queen Vashti for her impact on the common people of her time. Vashti was not a woman of God, but she did something that every Christian woman and man ought to applaud. This is why I include her as a lesser-known character, as she is among what we might call a marginal woman of impact in the book of Esther. Have you known someone, not a believer, who demonstrated moral excellence that can be similar to or better than a believer? Vashti is such an example.

The book of Esther is about the remarkable Jewish girl who helped to save her people in the days of King Ahasuerus (Xerxes). However, if it had not been for Vashti's action, Esther might not have providentially taken her place as queen.

The name Vashti means "beautiful woman." She must have been one of the most beautiful in the land to be chosen as queen ruling Persia and Media. She burst onto the pages of Bible history during Ahasuerus' third year of his reign when he had a celebration lasting 180 days, together with all the VIPs from the vast empire. The king then gave a seven-day feast for all the people in Susa, from great to small. The week-long event was marked with drinks of wine from golden goblets; each one was one-of-a-kind. On the seventh day, when the king was "merry with wine" (drunk), he sent his eunuchs to call Vashti to come before all the government officials "to show her beauty" (Esther 1:11).

But Vashti refused the king's request. No queen had ever done that before, and it sent shockwaves throughout the crowd. No doubt the king was embarrassed. It says he was "furious, and his anger burned within him" (v. 12). He called an emergency meeting with his closest officials—especially those well-versed in the law of the land—about what was to be done. Vashti didn't just refuse the king; she disobeyed orders and broke the law.

The advice given to the king was that unless he took drastic action, it would spark a women's liberation movement and affect all the households throughout the kingdom. They said it might cause all women to "despise their husbands in their eyes." The end of the story is that Vashti was removed as queen and was replaced with Esther. (Read the entire account of the rise of Esther and disposing of Vashti in Esther 1–2:17.)

The book of Esther is primarily the story of Esther, Mordecai, and the saving of the Jewish people from a holocaust. In speaking about Vashti, the main reason for the book should not be overshadowed. Nevertheless, her actions should not be passed over as insignificant.

There is no mention of God in the book of Esther, yet the providence of God shines through all the remarkable events still celebrated today by Jews as the Feast of Purim. What is also unusual in this story is that a heathen queen takes a bold public stand not to allow her beauty and her flesh to be paraded before a bunch of lustful eyes of drunken men.

It was not as though Vashti was a hired body or a beauty simply to wave at festivals before the people. Rather, she was the wife of King Ahasuerus, and she reigned with him over 127 provinces, from India to Ethiopia. Vashti knew as the First Lady of the land that her role was to display dignity, self-respect, and moral character. The king banished her from the kingdom, but her one-night moral stand demonstrated that she understood how a sovereign should act. It took such a vessel of honor to display moral character in a story about saving the Jews, whose highest honor belonged to Jehovah God.

We do not know what became of Vashti, but tradition and some sources say her name was also Amestris, and if this is so, she may have remarried. Esther 2:1 says that some time lapsed after the Vashti incident, and presumably she was still alive and living some place in the kingdom. If this is true, it shows that her husband did not banish her immediately after her refusal at the great festival. When Ahasuerus's anger subsided, his servants suggested they begin the search for a replacement, which eventually led to Esther as the next queen. Vashti moved on with her life. But she did make an impact.

APPLICATION

1. To paraphrase a Bible verse, "Men look upon a woman's outward appearance, but God looks at the heart of both the woman and the man."
2. Beauty may be skin deep, but moral behavior comes from deep inside a person's heart and soul.

REFLECTION

- Better to choose refusal than give oneself to expediency and market the flesh.
- There is great power at times in a simple "no." Bill Gaither said on a radio broadcast, "It can make a difference in our lives by what we say yes to and what we say no to."

- In good taste and in morality, saying yes to something often requires saying no to something or someone else.

15

Gomer

A WOMAN WHO BECAME A SERMON

BACKGROUND: Hosea 1:1–10; 3:1–5

KEY VERSE: *"Then the L*ORD *said to me, 'Go again, love a woman who is loved by a lover and is committing adultery, just like the love of the L*ORD *for the children of Israel…'"* (Hosea 3:1)

Gomer may not necessarily qualify as a lesser-known Bible character, but I include her because she is often overlooked. The prophet Hosea took Gomer as his wife as a living dramatic sermon illustration of how God felt about His people to whom Hosea was called to minister as God's messenger.

Bible scholars differ as to whether Hosea married Gomer when she was a harlot or whether she left her husband then went into harlotry. It seems to be the former, for Scripture says, "Go, take yourself a wife of harlotry" (Hosea 1:2).

Their children's names are significant to the prophecy of Hosea. Their names and meanings indicate what God thought about Israel. Hosea's first child was named Jezreel, which means "God will scatter." His second child was Lo-Ruhamah meaning "never known a father's pity." The third child was named Lo-Ammi meaning "not my people." The three names depict God's displeasure over Israel's conduct. This was not a parable but a reference to the reality of the nation's spiritual condition.

To get back his adulterous wife, Hosea buys Gomer from what we would call today her "pimp." Hosea's experience of Gomer's unfaithfulness was a reflection of how God felt about His people forsaking Him. Hosea's anguish over Gomer leaving him for a life of harlotry was parallel to God's anguish over Israel leaving Him to serve other gods. God commanded Hosea to take Gomer back, and she was to stay with him and no longer chase after another lover. This, too, was a reflection of God's mercy and love for His people. If a man could forgive, love, and restore a woman to their marriage, how much more is God's unfathomable love to forgive and restore His adulterous people.

Note how God uses the names of their children in depicting Israel's past backsliding and turns them into promises of the restoration of His people. Hosea 2:21–23 reads: "I will command the sky to send rain on the earth, and it will produce grain, grapes, and olives in Jezreel Valley. I will scatter the seeds and show mercy to Lo-Ruhamah. I will say to Lo-Ammi, "You are my people," and they will answer, "You are our God" (CEV).

This story of Hosea and Gomer is a message of God's far-reaching love for a people who strayed far from Him. It is a message to all prodigals, the Gomers, and others who have chosen to be like seed scattered in mud rather than the rich soil of God's creation.

Dr. G. Campbell Morgan, writing in *The Minor Prophets*, talks about the significance of this remarkable separation and restoration of a marriage in the book of Hosea. He states:

> Out of his heart of agony Hosea learned the nature of sin of his people. They were playing the harlot, spending God's gifts in lewd traffic with other lovers. Out of that agony he had learned how God suffers over the sins of His people, because of His undying love. Out of God's love, Hosea's new care for Gomer was born, and in the method God ordained for him with her, he discovers God's method with Israel. Out of all this process of pain, there came full confidence in the ultimate victory of love.[13]

APPLICATION

1. Hosea's message is about the danger of prosperity. Israel was in love with the things of the world as Gomer was in love with her

lovers; but within was rot and moral decay. Man looks on the outward appearance but God looks within the heart and soul.
2. The gospel of Jesus Christ has within it the power to save as well as the power to restore when the saved stray from Him.

REFLECTION

- Grace is not blind, but neither is it passive. It reaches the highest mountain of pride to save, and it reaches the lowest valley to lift.
- God is always the seeker. He does not give up on anyone who might give up on themselves.
- Grace is not a license to sin; rather it is meant to teach us "that, denying ungodliness and worldly lusts, we should live soberly, righteously, and godly in the present age" (Titus 2:12).

16

Tamar No. 1

GRACE GREATER THAN OUR SIN

BACKGROUND: Genesis 38:6–26

KEY VERSE: *"Judah the father of Perez and Zerah, whose mother was Tamar…"* (Matthew 1:3, NIV)

In the genealogy of Jesus, there is a mysterious story of deception, sin, and grace. There are two women named Tamar in the Bible. The second one is more well-known as the daughter of David, sister of Absalom, who was raped by her half-brother. But, the lesser-known Tamar, who appears first in the Bible, and is the one referenced in Matthew's genealogy, is the one I label here as Tamar No. 1.

This Tamar was a Canaanite woman whom Er, the son of Judah (Jacob's fourth son by Leah), married. The Bible says that Er was wicked in the sight of the Lord, and the Lord killed him (Genesis 38:7). The nature of his sin is not revealed.

According to Mosaic law, the next of kin, the brother of Er, was to marry Tamar to provide an heir for the deceased brother. Er's brother's name was Onan. He knew if he bore a son with Tamar, the child would not be considered his heir but his brother's. So Onan took measures to ensure Tamar would not conceive when having intercourse with her. This displeased the Lord, and the Lord killed Onan also (v. 10).

Judah's next son was too young to marry, so he told Tamar to wait until he was grown. But then, when Judah didn't keep his word about this marriage, she took matters into her own hands and devised a way to get pregnant. After Judah's wife died, Tamar put her devious plan into play. She put on a veil and disguised herself and then waited by the wayside when Judah came along at the sheepshearing time. Judah thought she was a prostitute and asked to have sex with her. However, this was not just about seduction or prostitution on Tamar's part.

Tamar was not an Israelite, but she knew the laws of Israel. As a widow, she had no other means of inheritance except through an heir. This heir would have to come from Judah. Her plan was so well thought out that she preplanned the terms before engaging in sex with Judah. Judah promised her a goat, but she wanted something more as a pledge than just the goat. She asked for his seal and cord and staff as collateral. Judah obliged. Unlike his pledge to give Tamar to his youngest son, Judah sought to make good on his pledge to this unnamed prostitute. However, when he tried to send her a goat, she was nowhere to be found. Three months later, Judah was told Tamar had "played the harlot" and was pregnant. He responded, "Bring her out and let her be burned!" (Genesis 38:24). Tamar then produced Judah's signet, cord, and staff, proving he was the father of her yet unborn child. Judah then confessed that he had done wrong, or right by Tamar, depending on which point of view is taken.

Twins were then born to Tamar—one was named Zerah and the other Perez, as noted in Matthew. Judah and Tamar's son Perez, birthed by a Jewish father and a Gentile mother and written in the genealogy of Jesus, powerfully demonstrates that the ancestry of both Jew and Gentile are part of the gospel story. Amazing grace—greater than our sin.

APPLICATION

1. As God's Word warns us, "Be sure your sin will find you out" (Numbers 23:23).
2. Desperation can cause wrongful acts. Tamar so desired a child from this family that she was willing to go to any length to bring it to pass. She resorted to a method that cannot be condoned, yet she felt her motive justified her actions.

REFLECTION

- Judah, an Israelite, was motivated to engage a woman as a prostitute out of sheer lust. But Tamar the Canaanite had a nobler motivation to bear a child from Judah's tribal family.
- Despite the birth of twins to Tamar and Judah in a manner that was questionable in every respect, God sovereignly produced an heir allowing grace to prevail to accomplish His purposes in the end. It may have not been done in God's perfect will but nevertheless in His permissive will.

17

Three Marys

WOMEN IN THE SERVICE OF THE LORD

BACKGROUND: Matthew 27:55–61,
Acts 12:8–18, Romans 16:1–16

KEY VERSE: *"And Mary Magdalene was there, and the other Mary, sitting opposite the tomb."* (Matthew 27:61); *"[Peter] came to the house of Mary, the mother of John whose surname was Mark, where many were gathered together praying."* (Acts 12:12); *"Greet Mary, who labored much for us."* (Romans 16:6)

Obviously, in the New Testament, Mary was a common and popular name of the time. Besides the famous mother of Jesus and Mary Magdalene, the three Marys I talk about here have very little information given about them apart from their names. But the very fact they are mentioned means they are worth exploring.

MARY NO. 1

The first Mary, referred to in Matthew as "the other Mary," was the wife of Clopas and the mother of James, the apostle. Her mention here is mainly because she was of the inner circle of women who followed Jesus and ministered to His material needs. She followed Him from Galilee, witnessed His death, and was among the group that anointed His body, saw the empty tomb, and hurried to tell of it. She is called "the other Mary" by Matthew (27:61) to distinguish her from Mary Magdalene.

MARY NO. 2, MOTHER OF JOHN MARK

This Mary's contribution included her son, John Mark, as a Jesus follower and the author of the Gospel account in his name. She might have been a wealthy widow with a large home, where many apostles and disciples most likely gathered for praise and worship. It was to her house that Peter came after experiencing a miraculous prison break. Peter knew the believers were praying for him, so he rushed to Mary's house for safety and prayer. Peter would have been familiar with Mary and her large house, and he seemed to have a special bond with her son Mark, calling him "my son" (1 Peter 5:13).

Mary No. 2 may have been the sister or aunt to Barnabas, who sold family land to contribute to the early church at a critical time. This would explain why Barnabas defended Mark when there was an issue between him and Paul about whether Mark was ready for full-time ministry.

This Mary's house was significant to what was called the "Jesus sect" when the early church was facing much persecution. As the believers came together, there was bonding and strengthening of each other. Mary was a steadfast woman who the leaders and people looked to as an example. The believers being in "one accord" on Pentecost carried over in the house meetings at Mary's place.

MARY NO. 3, OF ROME

Of the three women mentioned here, there is little information about this specific Mary. But she was one of the twenty-some saints Paul mentions and specifically names who helped him in various ways in spreading the gospel. Paul wrote in Romans 16:6, "Greet Mary who labored much for us."

This Mary may have adopted her Jewish name upon her conversion. She and Persis may have teamed up to be co-laborers for the believers in Rome, encouraging new converts and reaching the unconverted. In referring to both Mary and Persis, Paul used the same wording that they "labored much in the Lord," which may indicate they were a team working together. Women in the early church were a force to be reckoned with.

APPLICATION

1. Women's place in ministry began when Jesus elevated them above and beyond the much lesser role given them by men at that time.

Jewish culture was male-dominated. Jesus reversed much of this, and the three Marys were part of Jesus' legacy in this respect.
2. The fact that Jesus first appeared to women after His resurrection—we know Mary No. 1 was one of them—is remarkable because the Jewish Talmud stated that women's testimony was unreliable. Scripture proves otherwise.

REFLECTION

- Women were an essential and integral part of proclaiming the gospel following the death and resurrection of Jesus. They were then, and they are now.
- The women's "liberation movement" of the New Testament was that many worked for the Lord outside the home while not denouncing their domestic role.
- Jesus engaged women publicly, something unheard of in that day. Mary No. 1 was evidence of that. The home of Mary No. 2 was the center of power and fellowship for the church, both spiritually and physically. Paul did not hesitate to highlight the kingdom work of Mary No. 3.

18

Salome

A MODEL MOTHER

BACKGROUND: Matthew 27:56; Mark 15:38–16:8

KEY VERSE: *"When the Sabbath was over, Mary Magdalene, Mary the mother of James, and Salome bought spices so that they might go to anoint Jesus' body."* (Mark 16:1, NIV)

Salome and her husband, Zebedee, were followers of Jesus. They were devoted and godly parents of James and John, two of Jesus' twelve disciples. Salome was also a part of the itinerate group of women who helped Jesus during His ministry journeys.

Jesus spoke of the faithful women who followed Him, including Salome, calling them "daughters of Jerusalem" (Luke 23:28). She was devoted to Jesus and witnessed His crucifixion (Mark 15:40). Salome and a group of women that included Jesus' mother were the first to find the tomb empty. They then became the first evangelists reporting the news to the disciples, who did not believe them.

Salome's character as a mother is revealed when she appealed to Jesus to appoint her sons to "sit, one on Your right hand and the other on the left, in Your kingdom" (Matthew 20:21). This was an overly ambitious mother wanting the best for her sons. Jesus did not rebuke Salome directly for this request but instead redirected it by letting her know the cost to be paid before her sons could merit such a position in His kingdom. They both would die in martyrdom by serving Jesus after His ascension to heaven; James would be first and John last.

Besides Salome being too ambitious regarding her sons—for which she could be forgiven as a mother—she was a woman of undying devotion to Jesus. As a parent, she was unwavering in her faith and sacrifice toward her sons. Her husband, Zebedee, had a prosperous fishing business, where the sons were employed. When Jesus asked if they would follow Him and become fishers of men, they did not hesitate (Matthew 4:21); nor is there any indication that father and mother tried to persuade their sons otherwise.

Salome is a hidden treasure in plain sight, particularly when seeing her role in raising two sons who were willing to forsake all to not only follow Jesus but also share the Good News of the Messiah, regardless of the cost.

APPLICATION

1. I used to wonder how James and John could so readily leave the fishing business to follow Jesus. Perhaps their mother's influence may be at the root of it.
2. Salome, like many who followed Jesus, did not realize the sacrifices required to be a long-time follower. Many drop by the wayside. The price is too high for them.

REFLECTION

- When parents support the call of God in their children's life, they will share in the blessings that come because of that calling.
- Parents should be ambitious for their children in God's work rather than the opposite.
- One of the greatest antidotes against sin in a child's life are parents that instill in them a love for God and an example of godliness.

19

Anna

GROWING OLD GRACEFULLY

BACKGROUND: Luke 2:27–40

KEY VERSE: *"Now there was one, Anna, a prophetess…and this woman was a widow of about eighty-four years, who did not depart from the temple, but served God with fastings and prayers night and day."* (Luke 2:36,37)

Luke tells us Anna was a "prophetess," meaning she had great spiritual insight. She was widowed at an early age, having been married only seven years before she lost her husband; she must have then dedicated herself full-time to serving God in the temple. If Anna married as a virgin, she would have been in her late teens. If widowed seven years later, that might have made her about twenty-five years old. If she then moved into the temple, she would have been fasting twice a week as was the custom, praying daily and doing so for about sixty years. Indeed she grew old gracefully, without letting any grass grow under her feet.

During these years of service, Anna witnessed the event of Joseph and Mary bringing Jesus into the temple to be dedicated. When Simeon had finished praying for Mary and Jesus at His dedication, Anna had the great privilege to set her eyes on the Promised One.

Good things happen to those who remain faithful to the Lord. Anna anticipated the coming of the Messiah, and as a result, she was given the privilege of seeing Him in the flesh. She was an ordinary servant of the Lord, but her long days of consistent fasting and prayer were an extraordinary act of service. Sometimes it's not just the service we render to the Lord but how faithful we are to it throughout our lives that deserves notice.

Every pastor knows that the spiritual backbone of the congregation is the faithful members who, without fanfare, sit in their pew for every service. They worship, pray, give, listen to the Word, and quietly leave at the end of the service. You can always count on them being in attendance when able. Having been a pastor, I call them low-maintenance church members. They came to serve and not be served. They genuinely epitomize "the impact of ordinary people."

Anna's service changed after seeing Jesus in the temple. It was no longer about the One who was to come but about the One who had arrived. She testified to everyone who came into the temple about what she had witnessed: "She gave thanks to the Lord, and spoke of Him to all those who looked for redemption in Jerusalem" (Luke 2:38).

A true disciple has a personal relationship with Jesus Christ. I'm sure many who went to the temple to pray might have done so out of tradition and maybe even praying by rote. Not so of Anna.

God bless all those who make church attendance a habit. Yet, the church needs more than people filling a pew—it needs those whose hearts are full of love for God. We used to sing in church a hymn from 2 Timothy 1:12: "I know whom I have believed and am persuaded that He is able to keep that which I've committed unto Him against that day."

APPLICATION

1. Age, health, and whatever life transition we may be in has nothing to do with serving or not serving God. In each season of life, He gives us opportunities to use our gifts, talents, and influence to advance the kingdom of God.
2. Sometimes, it's hard to grow old gracefully due to health and other issues. Those who do leave a legacy of faithfulness, such as Anna, are entrusted with great revelations and special opportunities for service to God.

REFLECTION

- Our presence in service to the Lord is a testimony of the gospel that saves us but also keeps us at all times. As Spurgeon noted, "I feel that, if I could live a thousand lives, I would like to live them all for Christ, and even then, I would feel they were all too little a return for His great love for us."[14] The age on my driver's license does not tell me I have to slow down. Neither does yours.
- It is not just our faithfulness to God that is important, but God's faithfulness to us. That is why we serve Him.

20

Joanna

A WOMAN OF SUBSTANCE

BACKGROUND: Luke 8:1–3

KEY VERSE: *"And the twelve were with Him, and certain women who had been healed of evil spirits and infirmities—…and Joanna the wife of Chuza, Herod's steward…"* (Luke 8:1–3)

Joanna has an unusual bio. She was a woman of means married to Chuza, a man who held an important position in the government as a house steward of Herod the Tetrarch. It was remarkable that she was a part of the women who accompanied Jesus and the Twelve on their itinerant ministry. How was it that Joanna traveled with Jesus away from her household and husband, giving "substance" to supply and care for Him and the disciples' needs? There was a reason.

Jesus had healed Joanna. Though we're not given details, she received some physical healing that caused her to dedicate her time and expenses to following Jesus. After experiencing the healing touch of Jesus, how could she not give back in some way to express her love for Him? Having financial means, Joanna gave to the ministry of Jesus and His disciples.

Besides assisting the ministry, Joanna would have also had the opportunity to be a witness for Christ among the palace staff, her husband's coworkers, and probably the higher-ups. This is not just conjecture, for there is evidence that if there were "saints...who are of Caesar's household" (Philippians 4:22), there must have also been those of faith in Herod's household.

As a close follower of Jesus, Joanna might have been among the first to arrive at the burial site where Jesus' body was entombed. The Scripture states that women came to Jerusalem at the time of his death "from Galilee" (Luke 23:55,56). It does not say Joanna was in the group that "prepared spices and fragrant oils" for the body of the Lord, but it is likely, based on the chapter that follows.

The next day, the women returned to the tomb, and "they found the stone rolled away from the tomb. Then they went in and did not find the body of the Lord Jesus" (Luke 24:2,3). They might have assumed the body had been stolen rather than realizing they were indeed historical eyewitnesses to the resurrection of Jesus.

The women then told the eleven disciples what they saw, but the men did not believe them. Did the disciples reject the report because it was hard to believe or because the witnesses were women? Perhaps the latter, for the disciples said they considered what they said as "idle tales" (Luke 24:11).

Joanna might have been among the first to herald the resurrection of Jesus. Lockyer states: "Joanna, then, was the last at the cross, and among the first to witness the empty tomb to proclaim that the Lord whom she had so dearly loved was risen indeed. How much the cause of Christ owes to the consecrated Joanna!"[15]

APPLICATION

1. Those who consistently follow Jesus go through very dark times when He appears to be gone from their lives, but then He always reappears with resurrection power.
2. Joanna did not get her healing from Jesus then simply get on with her life. Her love for Jesus motivated her to follow Him in a substantive way.

REFLECTION

- When Joanna and the others saw that God had raised the body of Jesus, something miraculous arose in them. They were never the same.

- One of the greatest statements in the Word of God is that *Jesus rose from the dead.*
- At first, the tomb was a symbol of the end for the disciples. But then the empty grave was a sign of a new beginning, and it still is for those who believe in Jesus who is "alive forevermore" (Revelation 1:18).

21

Dorcas

RAISED TO LIFE

BACKGROUND: Acts 9:36–43

KEY VERSE: *"But Peter put them all out, and knelt down and prayed. And turning to the body he said, 'Tabitha, arise.' And she opened her eyes, and when she saw Peter she sat up."* (Acts 9:40)

By prayer in the name of Jesus, death obeyed Peter because Peter commanded life to enter a dead body. This was the first miracle of its kind in the early church.

Dorcas, also known as Tabitha, was a woman of God identified by many as "full of good works and charitable deeds" (Acts 9:36). Because of her reputation, after she became sick and died, two disciples, knowing Peter was nearby in Joppa, summoned him to Dorcas' house. We do not know whether the two unnamed disciples had faith for

Dorcas to be raised up from death. Probably not. There was no record of any miracle of this kind from the apostles.

When Peter arrived at the home of Dorcas, her friends showed Peter the clothing she had made for them. She was known in the community for her work with fabric and donating to those in need. (In earlier American history, and even in some other countries, Dorcas societies were formed to provide clothing to the poor as well as to support missions' endeavors worldwide.)

Peter asked the friends to leave the room so he could pray for Dorcas. Two things happened after Peter prayed: she opened her eyes, and she sat up. We can spiritualize things too much, but nevertheless, these two things happened: her eyes were opened when life came back into her, and because of this, she could sit and rise. We rarely see such physical resurrections today, but we do see spiritual resurrections. Whenever and wherever the gospel is preached, it can open eyes and can raise to new life those who are dead in their sins (Acts 26:18; Colossians 2:13).

I have spent sixty-plus years of my life helping to raise the spiritually and emotionally dead. I have loved speaking the Word to those walking dead men and women and witnessing them raised to a new way of living through Jesus Christ. I have never witnessed a person physically dead being brought to life, but I have seen those dead in their trespasses and sins brought to life when they put their trust in Christ.

What lessons can be learned from Dorcas? Yes, she was well spoken of because of her acts of kindness. But the larger message is that Jesus is "the resurrection and the life" (John 11:25). We are alive in Him!

APPLICATION

1. Open your eyes! Don't allow a disability or disease to blind you to the fact that God can still use you in your weaknesses and struggles.
2. Sit up! Sometimes we just need someone else's faith and encouragement to get out of bed and get on with our lives despite physical and emotional challenges.

REFLECTION

- In the same chapter in which Dorcas was raised from physical death, we read that Saul of Tarsus was raised from spiritual death. In both cases, they needed help after their miracle. Saul was led to Ananias for recovery, and for Dorcas, it was Peter who "gave her his hand and lifted her up." God did what only He could do in both miracles.
- After being brought to life, Dorcas no doubt continued her charity work rather than becoming some type of celebrity. Today we too often turn miracles into a circus act.

- It was Dorcas' sewing work that gave her notoriety. It's not just the sensational things we do that deserve notice; it's also the faithfulness in carrying out everyday works of charity.

22

Rhoda

SHE LEFT PETER OUTSIDE THE GATE!

BACKGROUND: Acts 12:1–18

KEY VERSE: *"As Peter knocked at the door of the gate, a girl named Rhoda came to answer."* (Acts 12:13)

Rhoda was a girl working in the house of Mary, the mother of John Mark, the evangelist. Her name, in Greek, means "Rose," and we can imagine she was beautiful in character and service as a domestic servant in the house where there were many visitors she would have waited on.

One night, a serious prayer meeting was taking place in the house of Mary on behalf of Peter, who was in prison and perhaps facing execution. During the prayer time, Peter received an unexpected but welcomed visitor—an angel on assignment. With two guards by his side, Peter was asleep when this angel poked him on the side with the instruction to "arise quickly!" The angel then led Peter safely out of the prison unseen.

Peter traveled to Mary's house. When Rhoda heard a knock on the door and Peter's voice, she was so excited that she left him standing there as she ran back to tell everyone at the prayer meeting that Peter was at the door. They told her she was crazy (Acts 12:12–15). But Rhoda was just the messenger.

The story of Rhoda represents all believers who, when they pray for something or someone and then experience the answer to prayer, may not believe the answer, even if it is staring them in the face. The entire prayer group, gathered on behalf of Peter, did not believe Rhoda. Of course, when they saw Peter in the flesh, they knew it was an answer to their prayers.

Often God sends His answers to prayer through the most unlikely ones involved. Rhoda was just an ordinary servant who found herself in the middle of a miracle of answered prayer. I have often found that it is the least likely Christians who are the ones to see up close God's workings on behalf of someone needing deliverance, as happened to Peter. I encourage newborn converts to be bold in asking God for their needs or the needs of others because their faith is simple, and they need to see *signs and wonders* to strengthen them on their new journey with the Lord. Keep praying and believing.

APPLICATION

1. Don't pray unless you expect an answer.
2. As Peter kept knocking at the door, so we ought to keep knocking and believing for answers to our prayers.

REFLECTION

- Pray out of desperation! The greater and more desperate the need, the more fervent the prayers should be. Always pray with an open book, the Bible, centered on the promises of God.
- Prayers made out of great need are the type we pray for most often. Praise and thanksgiving after answered prayer are just as important. Anyone who can breathe can pray: "Let everything that has breath praise the LORD" (Psalm 150:6).
- "We are to ask with a beggar's humility, to seek with a servant's carefulness, and knock with the confidence of a friend."[16] (D. L. Moody)

23

Damaris

A SEED OF FAITH

BACKGROUND: Acts 17:16–34

KEY VERSE: *"And when they heard of the resurrection of the dead, some mocked, while others said, 'We will hear you again on this matter.' ... However, some men joined him and believed, among them Dionysius the Areopagite, a woman named Damaris, and others with them."* (Acts 17:32–34)

Some preachers, especially missionaries, often minister where the soil is hard and the seed of the Word is stubbornly resisted. This was the case when Paul preached in Athens on Mars Hill, a place where his message was mocked, and others politely dismissed it as unworthy of a response. After Paul's preaching, however, a man named Dionysius and a woman Damaris and "others with them" believed and were converted.

We know nothing about Damaris, but we can rightly say she most likely was a Gentile because she was in Athens. Her conversion as a believer was a testimony that the gospel message can bear fruit in the most unlikely places and with the most unlikely people. Damaris's conversion, to me, was a big deal because of where it happened.

Athens was the capital of Attica, one of the Greek states. It was the center of what today might be called liberalism in thinking and science, literature, and art. Mars Hill was located some short distance from the city center. Paul happened to be there, having escaped from Thessalonica, where his preaching resulted in a mob gathering. He left Silas and Timothy behind with arrangements to meet them in Athens. It was a safer place to be as it had a reputation for law and order. There were no plans, it seems, for Paul to make Athens a preaching point.

As Paul waited for his traveling companions, Acts 17 says that "his spirit was provoked within him when he saw that the city was given over to idols" (v. 16). He then spoke in the local synagogue to Jews and Gentile worshipers, who gave him a less than enthusiastic reception, calling his preaching "babbling."

When Paul spoke to Jews, his message began with Moses and ended with Jesus. Here among the Gentiles, he began with the God of creation and finished with a message of judgment and the resurrection. The latter was apparently new to many and some mocked, while others wanted to hear more (Acts 17:32). Nevertheless, he departed Athens, and the last we hear of his visit, there was the mention of Damaris among a small group who embraced Paul's gospel message. It's unclear why Paul mentions Damaris, but she represents how seeds of faith were planted in a pagan city. Our witness of the gospel can take root in anyone's heart.

APPLICATION
1. Those like the Athenians bear witness that man is created with spiritual hunger, and they will seek it wherever and in whatever way they can find it. Paul said such people may "grope for Him and find Him, though He is not far from each one of us" (Acts 17:27).
2. The message can still bear fruit even when it seems no one is responding to the gospel.

REFLECTION
- If there are only a few lights in a dark place, others may find their way to that light that brings hope. The darker the place, the more important is the Light.
- One of the hardest places to preach is where it's been given over to a New Age kind of religion.
- Some are on the wrong road because it's the only road they know until someone shows them a better way. Damaris found it.

24

Phoebe

PURE AND RADIANT AS THE MOON

BACKGROUND: Romans 16:1–16

KEY VERSE: *"I commend you to Phoebe our sister, who is a servant of the church in Cenchrea…for indeed she has been a helper of many and of myself also."*
(Romans 16:1,2)

Paul would disagree that Phoebe is among the lesser-knowns, for she certainly was not to him. But when I asked some friends to list names of Bible women, most did not know her name or why she was on Paul's list of remembrance. Phoebe was at the top of the list of almost thirty names Paul mentions in this passage. In Romans 16:1,2, Paul describes Phoebe and what she meant to the members of the early church.

Paul refers to Phoebe as "our sister" and as "a servant of the church." She is said to have conducted business with church members and was "a helper of many and myself also."

Phoebe's name means "pure or radiant as the moon," which is a very endearing characterization of the kind of person she was, and it's no wonder she was on the top of Paul's list. She was probably first encountered by Paul in Cenchrea, a town east of Corinth. In that town, Paul, for reasons unknown, shaved his head as part of a Jewish vow (Acts 18:18). Whatever that vow was, Phoebe may have helped Paul when he was in some kind of trouble. He may have been sick and thus attended to by Phoebe. She was a businesswoman and may have also helped Paul financially. Scholars believe she may have delivered Paul's epistle to the believers in Rome.

Paul's reference to her as "our sister" meant she was a sister in the Lord. We do not know when she became a member of the family of God. The use of the word "our" referred to her status in the church. In addition, she was called "a servant in the church"—her home church in Cenchrea. The word "servant" is taken from the Greek word *diakonos*, from which we get the word "deaconess." She may have been the first such deaconess of the early church.

Paul uses his epistle to the Romans to ask the church to accord her the right hand of fellowship, and to "assist her in whatever business she has need of you" (v. 2). Entrusting such an important letter to the believers in Rome shows what high esteem Phoebe held in Paul's eyes.

APPLICATION

1. The church then and now would not be what it is without the ministry of key women who selflessly labor for the Lord and leaders of the church.
2. Many women assume there is no place in the ministry for them for a simple reason: they don't ask where and who they can serve in the church or a ministry.

REFLECTION

- Paul said Phoebe was a helper, and evidently, she became so successful that she needed helpers to help herself.
- Growing up, I saw women who wanted a prominent position in the church or they would not serve. It's better that they didn't, with such an attitude.
- The more we do for God, the more He can trust us to be given more responsibility. Phoebe was a businesswoman and traveled, which meant she could deliver Paul's epistle to the church in Rome. It may not seem to be a big deal in retrospect, but it was at the time.

25

Priscilla

THE STRONG NOT-SO-SILENT PARTNER

BACKGROUND: Acts 18:1–3,18–27

KEY VERSE: *"And [Paul] found a certain Jew named Aquila, born in Pontus, who had recently come from Italy with his wife Priscilla…So, because he was of the same trade, he stayed with them and worked; for by occupation they were tentmakers."* (Acts 18:2,3)

During Paul's ministry, he often worked with a couple named Aquila and Priscilla. In his lengthy list of people who assisted him in his missionary work, the fact that Aquila and Priscilla were among the first ones he sent greetings to may be significant (Romans 16:3). They were instrumental in helping the eloquent teacher/speaker Apollos when they "explained to him the way of God more accurately"

THE IMPACT OF ORDINARY PEOPLE

(Acts 18:26). They also had a house church in Ephesus (1 Corinthians 16:19).

We don't know a lot about this couple but what we do know is that they were ministry partners. Today in certain circles, some still question the place for women in ministry. I differ with that, and seemingly so does Paul. Of the five times this couple is mentioned in Scripture, twice Priscilla is mentioned first (Acts 18:18; Romans 16:3). I take it from this that she was the strong, not-so-silent partner.

My mother was very much a partner with my father in pastoring churches. When my dad got sick, at times quite frequently (he died at age fifty-three), my mother filled the pulpit in his place. However, she never felt it was her place to be involved in the government of the church.

In saying that husband and wife are involved in ministry, it should not be assumed that both have a public ministry. My wife, Cindy, has always been the behind-the-scenes presence in all aspects of my ministry. We never made any decisions about our personal lives or ministry unless it was together. Because my wife prefers to be in the background, it's often assumed she's silent. It's not so when it comes to the challenges I face and when I get too ahead of myself or I am about to make an unwise decision. I can always depend on her to give me a timely word of warning, encouragement, or in her own way, be my prophetic partner. Those close to us know that my wife understands there is a time to be quiet and a time to speak. Some of her nuggets of wisdom make me laugh while at the same time make a necessary point.

Lockyer writes about why Priscilla is always paired with her husband: "It is difficult to separate her place on a pedestal of her own. Their two hearts beat together. Harmoniously, they labored together...they walked as one for they had mutually agreed to put God first."[17]

The point in choosing Priscilla as a person—a woman—of impact is because there are people who fulfill their calling in more private ways, like my wife. They are often viewed as ordinary servants of the Lord. Some women are called into public ministry and are gifted teachers/preachers, especially to women in the body of Christ. Some women make an impact behind the scenes. However, the publicity-seeking women in ministry are ones I avoid, if possible.

Growing up in the church and having been a pastor and parachurch leader, it's been my experience that the work of God goes forward because of the service of women, both publicly and privately.

APPLICATION

1. A woman who teaches the Word as a gifted teacher should not be accepted or rejected because she is a woman but because she shares the truth of God's Word to all.

2. Priscilla was part of a team with her husband and therefore was probably a good example in the church to single women and men who may not have such role models.

REFLECTION

- Because Paul lists Priscilla's name first in Romans 16:3, she might have had the greater ministry gift; if so, her husband is an example of how such husbands should support their wives.
- She and her husband were tentmakers alongside Paul, and he stayed in their home, and that is when they might have come to the Lord (Acts 18:2,3).

26

Julia

CALLED TO BE A SAINT

BACKGROUND: Romans 16:1–16

KEY VERSE: *"Greet Philologus and Julia, Nereus and his sister, and Olympas, and all the saints who are with them."* (Romans 16:15)

The names written by Paul in Romans chapter 16 were converts who came to believe in the Savior. It is too bad we don't know how they came to Christ, whether through the witness of Paul or someone else. But we do know that evangelism in the early church was similar to today in many aspects. One similarity is that in the early church days, many came to Christ through a relationship with a believer that we might call *friendship evangelism*. If a new person went to a house church, it would have been by an association with a believer that invited them.

Paul greets Philologus and Julia, who might have been brother and sister but more likely husband and wife. One may have found Christ first and led the other and even other family members to faith. In those days, household salvations were not unusual. In their society, people were much less individualistic and often were a part of a strong family unit.

Some believe Julia and her family might have been among the higher class due to wealth, social connections, or other reasons. One commentator describes her as "a member of one of the great houses of Rome" and "a member of the imperial court and therefore among the saints to be found in Caesar's household,"[18] which Paul speaks of in other cases. From Paul's writing, we know that in Thessalonica "prominent women" joined the new Jesus movement (Acts 17:12).

We don't know for sure what Julia's status was in Roman society but we do know that Paul held her in high esteem. Christianity had made inroads into all aspects of culture and society life. From Paul's writing, we know that in Thessalonica, "prominent women" joined the new Jesus movement (Acts 17:12).

It might seem unusual and remarkable that someone of Julia's stature would be a part of what might be called the underground Christian church at the time. But Christianity is the only religion that can satisfy a spiritually hungry person. Many households practiced rituals to gods that were supposed to protect them. There was no personal devotion involved in such practices, and it left people void and empty of a relationship with a living God. This made the Christian religion attractive to genuine seekers after truth and God. The communion meal was especially well-received because it provided a mixture of fellowship, ritual through the communion table, and worship. Yet even the Christian religion can be turned into a ritual. Paul had to bring correction to those who turned the communion service into a feast instead of a celebration of Christ's death.

This is a background to how Julia and others in the early church might have come to Christ and become part of the early church. What other lessons can be found in the early church converts that might apply to today?

APPLICATION

1. Just as Jesus had followers with "substance," meaning some level of wealth especially women, the same is true of Paul's ministry. God places wealth in some believers' hands so they can use it to spread the gospel.
2. God also uses a person's wealth of connections, influence, and even social standing when they are Christians for the glory of God.

REFLECTION

- One of the most remarkable statements Paul makes is when he sends greetings to the church in Philippi, particularly to those "who are of Caesar's household" (Philippians 4:22). Politics and working for government leaders does not have to be doing Satan's work. The darker the place, the greater is the power of light.
- What an encouragement it must have been to Julia and the many others named on his list when he stated, "I am not ashamed of the gospel of Christ" (Romans 1:16). Rome was not an easy place to live out the gospel, and today those in countries closed to the gospel are still encouraged by the book of Romans.
- One of the highest testimonies one could have then, as well as today, is to be referred to as a "saint"—one set apart for the cause of Christ.

27

Chloe

PART OF THE PROBLEM OR THE SOLUTION

BACKGROUND: 1 Corinthians 1:10–17

KEY VERSE: *"For it has been declared to me concerning you, my brethren, by those of Chloe's household, that there are contentions among you."* (1 Corinthians 1:11)

Paul gets to the point right away in his letter to the church in Corinth, whom he refers to as "my brethren." We don't know if Chloe was in the middle of this "contention" going on in the church or not, nor do we know exactly what the issue was. Was she part of the problem or part of the solution? I sense that she was not part of the problem; if she were, why would she report it? The contentious ones usually don't declare their actions to such a man of God as Paul.

We don't have to speculate about the contentions Paul addresses. The church seemed divided because of which leader they identified with: were they following Paul, Apollos, Cephas, or Christ (1 Corinthians 1:12)? In those days, the church was so new and there were not many pastor-teachers to follow. As a result, the church was divided over which leader they revered more than another instead of following Christ. I like to think this lifting up of one minister over another had its root in a love for the man of God they felt brought them to know the gospel. However, instead of accepting each other's preference in who they followed, most turned it into celebrity worship—a problem we still face today.

As Paul continues his teaching in this letter, he writes about the foolishness of man's wisdom. This leads me to wonder if the root of the contention was a judgment of Paul as inferior. In comparison to Apollos, known for being a very eloquent speaker, Paul's speaking-teaching style, or eloquence of speech, may have been viewed as less powerful or engaging. The churches he is writing to in Corinth may not have understood the importance of his letter. Paul sensed this and wrote, "And I, brethren, when I came to you, I did not come with excellence of speech or of wisdom declaring to you the testimony of God" (1 Corinthians 2:1).

I served as pastor with my brother David and another man, the late Bob Phillips. We were a threefold pastoral team taking turns preaching, each of us once a week. We honored each other's ministry gifts. A man who attended all the services once stopped me while coming out of the church and said to me, "You're my favorite preacher." I smiled and thanked him. A week later, I overheard him saying the same to my brother. Then later, I saw him privately talking to Pastor Phillips. I didn't know what was said, but I had a good guess. I was going to go and rebuke him. But I felt the Lord speak to me: "He went to You, David, and Pastor Bob. Leave him alone, and eventually, maybe he'll make me his favorite preacher."

Today, in many evangelical circles, there is the cult of personality. Whatever Chloe and her household did, we can thank them for helping to raise the issue of favoritism in the church. Paul was able to set the record straight as he wrote in 1 Corinthians 2:2: "For I determined not to know anything among you except Jesus Christ and Him crucified." If this is understood, we will not have "favorites" in the church because Jesus will be so high and lifted up, all others will become eclipsed in the light of His glory and grace.

APPLICATION

1. Let the world have its celebrities and let the church have its servants and shepherds.
2. Paul considered jealousy, favoritism, and the exaltation of men or women in the church as carnality. He writes in 1 Corinthians 3:1 to the

THE IMPACT OF ORDINARY PEOPLE

entire church in Corinth, including Chloe's household, that they were still "babes in Christ." The church then was young in the faith. Since we benefit from learning from that church, let us be a part of the solution to bring unity to the church and not a part of its problem. I'd like to think this is what Chloe wanted.

REFLECTION

- Whatever the contentions were in the Corinthian church, they were serious enough that they served as the basis for both of Paul's letters to these believers. Another important admonition Paul sent to the church was this: "Your faith should not be in the wisdom of men but in the power of God" (1 Corinthians 2:5). On this the entire church should stand.
- God blesses a church or a ministry that is in "one accord" (Acts 1:14). If you find a church like this, join it.

28

Euodia & Syntyche

CALLED TO UNITY

BACKGROUND: Philippians 4:1–9

KEY VERSE: *"I implore Euodia and I implore Syntyche to be of the same mind in the Lord."* (Philippians 4:2)

It takes only two names and a brief instruction from the apostle Paul to guess other words he is implying when addressing Euodia and Syntyche. Words such as strife, division, disunity, discord, and perhaps jealousy come to mind. One or more of these words may have compelled Paul to "implore" Euodia and Syntyche to heal whatever was the cause of a difference between them.

The message Paul shares in this letter to the churches in Philippi addresses how the situation between these two people can be corrected and how the church should function as brothers and sisters in the Lord. In Philippians 2:2, Paul writes, "Fulfill my joy by being like-minded, having the same love, being of one accord, of one mind." And again in 3:16, "Nevertheless, to the degree that we have already attained, let us walk by the same rule, let us be of the same mind."

Because disunity still happens in churches and between those in the family of God, it is well worth a closer look at what might have been the problem between Euodia and Syntyche in the church in Philippi. We are not told what the issue was between them. But Paul does say they should be of one mind "in the Lord." They might have had different political or cultural opinions, but when it came to the things of God, they were challenged to be of "one mind." Could the issue have been about works versus grace, jealousy, or leadership difference?

Lockyer writes of this: "A humorist has suggested that because of the strife between these sisters they should have been called *Odious* and *Soon-touchy*. It was sad that there was this difference of opinion, and more tragic still that divisions have kept Christians apart all down the ages."[19]

The lesson here cuts to the heart of issues that have been in the church since the beginning. Differences between well-intended persons in the body of Christ will continue, but the critical question is how they are handled. Often minor issues become major when they become more of a matter of who is right rather than right versus wrong.

APPLICATION

1. Speaking "the truth in love" among mature believers is the standard of resolving differences. Strive for unity and, if not, agree that there is disagreement without hurt or animosity.
2. The devil loves to have the body of Christ be in division. He sits back and watches one believer attack another, as they do his work for him.

REFLECTION

- Jealousy is often behind differences between believers.
- One can have a preference in a matter without being stubborn. John Calvin said, "Matters non-essential should not be the basis of argument among Christians."
- When something similar takes place in the body of Christ, as it did for these two women, unity needs to give way to the Spirit over the flesh.

29

Eunice

A GODLY HERITAGE

BACKGROUND: 2 Timothy 1:1–5

KEY VERSE: *"I am reminded of your sincere faith, which first lived in your grandmother Lois and in your mother Eunice and, I am persuaded, now lives in you also."* (2 Timothy 1:5, NIV)

When it comes to the impact of Eunice raising Timothy in the Lord, one must also consider the influence of Timothy's grandmother, Lois. Paul considered their influence as a side-by-side endeavor.

Eunice means "conquering well" or "victory." The root word in Greek is *nike*, as is used in the modern, world-famous shoe company. Eunice certainly lived up to her name in bringing up her son to become an evangelist, coworker of apostle Paul, and recipient of two of Paul's epistles. When you add a God-fearing grandmother to the mix, Timothy had quite a heritage.

Timothy was given a double gift: a mother who made known to him the gift of salvation and a grandmother who taught him from the Scriptures. Sometimes in these writings, I have quoted Proverbs 22:6: "Train up a child in the way he should go, and when he is old he will not depart from it." This Scripture's importance cannot be overemphasized.

Matthew Henry wrote on Proverbs 22:6 that children needed to be trained "as soldiers, who are taught to handle their arms, keep rank, and observe the word of command. Train them up…in the way they should go, the way in which, if you love them, you would have them go."[20] Timothy is a great example of this, as well as Eunice, his mother.

Paul likely led Timothy's mother and grandmother to the Lord, which is why he may have referred to him as his "beloved son" in the faith. Because mother and grandmother were Jewesses, they would have brought up Timothy in the Old Testament teachings, and under Paul's influence, introduced him to Jesus' teaching.

My mother raised two sons who became preachers, and I know how blessed she was to see how the Lord used my brother and me. She would have known how Eunice felt when Paul saw in her son the gift of an evangelist (2 Timothy 4:5) and encouraged him in the use of it. Solomon wrote, "And let her who bore you rejoice" (Proverbs 23:25). I am sure Timothy's mother did.

APPLICATION
1. In a godly upbringing, the child is intended to be released to God like a bird out of a nest.
2. Timothy seems to have begun his ministry in his early youth, resulting from the spiritual schooling at home, enabling him to step into the responsibilities Paul assigned to him.

REFLECTION
- Eunice rejoiced that Timothy went into the ministry. However, such a child does not deserve special treatment over other siblings as Joseph was favored by his father, Jacob.
- Children should be encouraged in how God is calling them individually, not by the desire of the parents.
- Children given a spiritual heritage should give thanks to God for such a gift.

30

Apphia

WELCOMING A PRODIGAL

BACKGROUND: Philemon 1:1–25

KEY VERSE: *"Paul, a prisoner of Christ Jesus…to the beloved Apphia, Archippus our fellow soldier, and to the church in your house."* (Philemon 1:1,2)

I love this epistle of Paul, a personal letter written to Philemon about Onesimus, a runaway slave belonging to Philemon. Apphia may have been Philemon's wife and might be one of the least known women in the New Testament. But there is a moment in this letter that makes her very significant, at least to me.

I love this story of redemption and forgiveness; it's another version of a prodigal returning home, only in this case it was not a son but a slave returning. I have worked with hundreds of Onesimuses in my lifetime, and I know their stories, especially how they run from their past. I also know who they run from: a spouse, a parent, family, and friends. I know the challenge Philemon faced in whether to accept back a prodigal who desires to return.

Onesimus becomes a runaway slave and travels to Rome probably to hide. There, by some unknown circumstances, he ends up with Paul, who was under house arrest and is permitted visitors. Onesimus would have known about Paul through his association with his slave owner.

Paul leads Onesimus to Christ (note verse 10, "whom I have begotten while in my chains") and disciples him over some unknown time period. We know this because Paul mentions that Onesimus ministered to him, perhaps referring to the Christian fellowship they shared.

However, knowing Onesimus was a fugitive, Paul convinces him to go back to his master voluntarily. This was a major step for a slave and proof of life transformation and understanding of God's grace. The return is even more remarkable because Onesimus had stolen from Philemon, undoubtedly to finance his escape.

My favorite part of this story is envisioning when Onesimus walks onto Philemon's property, and probably another slave announces his presence. Might it have been Apphia who was the first to greet him and welcome him? I picture her accepting Onesimus back as a mother might. Then Philemon reads Paul's letter: "yet for love's sake I rather appeal to you...for my son Onesimus,...who once was unprofitable to you, but now is profitable to you and to me. I am sending him back. You therefore receive him, that is, my own heart..." (Philemon 1:9–12).

What a letter of recommendation on behalf of a runaway slave. Paul remarkably refers to him as "my son." We don't know the details of what happened next. However, William Barkley's commentary on Philemon states that Onesimus eventually became a bishop in the church, which meant Philemon gave the returning slave his freedom. It doesn't take much imagination to think what part Apphia might have had in this—another version of a prodigal received back as a "beloved brother" (Philemon 1:15).

APPLICATION

1. Paul mentioning Apphia in this letter shows how it takes the entire church body to help heal the brokenness of prodigals who return.
2. When Paul wrote, "If he has wronged you or owes anything, put that on my account" (v. 18), what a wonderful picture that is of what Christ did for us on the cross.

REFLECTION

- Paul's mention of Apphia at the beginning of his letter demonstrates that she and her husband Philemon were probably a team regarding spiritual matters. So it should be in a marriage.

- Paul referring to Apphia as "our beloved" signifies her importance to this story. As noted previously, she may have been the first to lovingly greet Onesimus on his return.
- It is good to see how Paul and Jesus lifted the importance of women in the Bible stories.

CONCLUSION

Women in Bible days often did not have the status they do now, although Jesus, and later Paul and the early church, raised the level of their importance. But even in Israel of the Old Testament, women were held in much higher esteem and position than in neighboring heathen nations, where they were subject to degrading positions. Esther had importance thrust upon her, and we know of other prominent names as Deborah, Sarah, Rebekah, Bathsheba, Jezebel, and others. But for every known woman, there were as many more lesser-knowns as I have written here.

The Old Testament gives us a sad understanding of polygamy, and at the time Moses wrote the Law, it was virtually accepted and practiced by the children of Israel. The Law did try to limit multiple marriages and concubines. But as covered in some of these chapters, we read about both its degrading effect on women while at the same time some remarkable stories of godly women who rose above it, even while being the victim of such sins.

In the Gospels, Jesus showed special attention to women, which was reflected in how they were drawn to Him and His teaching. Paul might not have been as successful in his missionary journeys preaching the gospel and planting churches without the involvement of various lesser-known women.

The lessons Bible women give us are a significant contribution to our discipleship growth. My prayer is that you will feel inspired and instructed about their importance in the home, the church, the community, and in some cases, their worldwide influence.

I have always given women my respect for the service they do to expand God's kingdom. This comes from witnessing my mother being an outreach evangelist running a coffee house ministry in Greenwich Village, Manhattan, in the 1960s. Before that, I recall her giving out food to the homeless who knocked on our door. My mother also led a youth group in our church and did pulpit preaching when my father, the pastor, got unexpectedly sick. In all of this, my mother was a behind-the-scenes and lesser-known worker in the vineyard of the Lord. As I write this, I realize that my mother, who is now in heaven, inspired me to write this book. I have dedicated it to her memory for her impact on my life and her service to God's kingdom.

NOTES

1. Myron S. and Esther Augsburger, *How to Be a Christ-Shaped Family* (Wheaton, IL: Victor Books, 1994), 51.
2. Martin Luther, *Selections from Table Talk* (Classic Reprint), (London: FB &c Limited, 2018).
3. Matthew Henry, "Genesis 4:20," *Matthew Henry Complete Commentary on the Whole Bible.* <studylight.org/commentaries/mhm/genesis-4.html>.
4. *Illustrated Dictionary of the Bible* (Nashville, TN: Thomas Nelson, 2003).
5. Herbert Lockyer, *All the Men of the Bible / All the Women of the Bible* (Grand Rapids, MI: Zondervan Publishing House, 2005), 40.
6. C. T. Studd, "Only One Life, 'Twill Soon Be Past" <tinyurl.com/4wm344sr>.
7. Quoted in *Charles F. Stanley, Charles Stanley's Handbook for Christian Living: Biblical Answers to Life's Tough Questions* (Nashville, TN: Thomas Nelson, 2008), 490.
8. Lockyer, *All the Men of the Bible / All the Women of the Bible*, 287.
9. Serena Dyksen, *She Found His Grace: A True Story of Hope, Love, and Forgiveness After Abortion* (Newberry, FL: Bridge-Logos, 2020).
10. Billy Graham, *Unto the Hills: A Daily Devotional* (Nashville, TN: Thomas Nelson, 2010), 147.
11. Lockyer, *All the Men of the Bible / All the Women of the Bible*, 38.
12. *Matthew Henry Study Bible-KJV* (Peabody, MA: Hendrickson Publishers, 2010).

13. G. Campbell Morgan, *The Minor Prophets: The Men and Their Messages* (New York: Fleming H. Revell Co., 1960).
14. *The Complete Works of C. H. Spurgeon*, Volume 48: Sermons 2760 to 2811 (Harrington, DE: Delmarva Publications, Inc., 2013).
15. Lockyer, *All the Men of the Bible / All the Women of the Bible*, 79.
16. Dwight L. Moody, *Prevailing Prayer: What Hinders It?* (Chicago, IL: F. H. Revell, 1884), 92.
17. Lockyer, *All the Men of the Bible / All the Women of the Bible*, 122.
18. Ibid.
19. Ibid., 55.
20. Matthew Henry, "Proverbs 22:6," *Matthew Henry Complete Commentary on the Whole Bible*. <studylight.org/commentaries/eng/mhm/proverbs-22.html>.

ALSO AVAILABLE FROM BRIDGE-LOGOS

YOUR FIRST STEP TO FREEDOM
Don Wilkerson

This instructional and informative book is written for those who want to help someone that is struggling with an addiction. For those struggling with a life-controlling problem, for church leaders, youth ministers, families, and friends of an addict, this book has been written for you.

With over 50 years of experience and seeing firsthand that people do not know how to help those suffering with an addiction, Don Wilkerson has written this book to help. Find useful guidance on:

- Taking the first step toward freedom
- Ministering to families of addicts
- Steps toward intervention for loved ones
- How to avoid a relapse
- From denial to decision
- And much more

ISBN: 978-1-61036-214-6

ALSO AVAILABLE FROM BRIDGE-LOGOS

GIVING HOPE AN ADDRESS
Julie Wilkerson Klose

For sixty years, the faith-based ministry of Teen Challenge has been bringing hope to those bound by drug and life-controlling addictions. Since the very first Teen Challenge Center opened its doors in Brooklyn, New York, the ministry has grown to 1,400 Centers across 122 nations.

Julie Wilkerson Klose, the daughter of Don Wilkerson and niece of David Wilkerson, grew up in the ministry of Teen Challenge. Julie is an educator and writer. She began her writing career as a regular contributor to a political website focusing on cultural issues from a Christian perspective, with a special passion for the pro-life movement.

www.JulieKlose.com

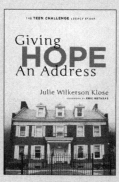

ISBN: 978-1-61036-472-0

ALSO AVAILABLE FROM BRIDGE-LOGOS

SHE FOUND HIS GRACE
Serena Dyksen with Julie Klose

When Serena Dyksen heard the news that over 2,200 babies' remains were found on the property of abortion doctor Ulrich "George" Klopfer, her whole body went numb from shock. She began to sob tears of grief. "Is my baby one of those remains?" she questioned. Dr. Klopfer performed her abortion when she was just thirteen years old. Just months before, Serena had decided to share her abortion story. After watching one of the last scenes in the pro-life movie Unplanned, she felt it was time to share the hope and healing God had done in her life. Serena's story reads like a traumatic tale: a childhood of dysfunction, rape, abortion at thirteen years old, a pregnant teenager at the age of sixteen, and health issues.

ISBN: 978-1-61036-249-8

Facebook.com/shefoundhisgrace
Instagram.com/she_found_his_grace
Pinterest.com/sdyksen
SerenaDyksen.com

ALSO AVAILABLE FROM BRIDGE-LOGOS

HELD
Melissa Eadie

Melissa Eadie was first diagnosed with cancer at the tender age of 14. While her peers were experiencing high school, the latest trends, and youthful ambitions, Melissa became familiar with the four corners of her hospital room. For the next 10+ years, "cancer" was a part of her everyday vocabulary. Tragically, her second diagnosis at 19 resulted in the loss of her right leg. A two-time cancer survivor and above knee amputee, Melissa's life is the definition of strength and perseverance, but she knows that victory includes the painful fight to the finish line. More than just a memoir, Melissa walks you through her vulnerable, "diary" moments in the process of growth, grieving, and forgiveness. Her story will lead you to the God that wraps you in love and shows you what it means to be ... Held.

ISBN: 978-1-61036-265-8

Instagram.com/@MellyDoesLife

ALSO AVAILABLE FROM BRIDGE-LOGOS

BEAUTY FROM ASHES
Donna Sparks

In a transparent and powerful manner, the author reveals how the Lord took her from the ashes of a life devastated by failed relationships and destructive behavior to bring her into a beautiful and powerful relationship with Him. The author encourages others to allow the Lord to do the same for them.

Donna Sparks is an Assemblies of God evangelist who travels widely to speak at women's conferences and retreats. She lives in Tennessee.

www.story-of-grace.com

www.facebook.com/donnasparksministries/

www.facebook.com/AuthorDonnaSparks/

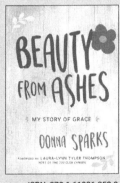

ISBN: 978-1-61036-252-8

ALSO AVAILABLE FROM BRIDGE-LOGOS

FEARLESS
Angela Donadio

What do Jochebed, Rahab, Abigail, the woman at the well, the woman with the issue of blood, and Priscilla have in common? Find your fearlessness in their stories.

This 6-session Bible study will help you to:

- **Stand Up** / Develop God-confidence to step into your unique calling.
- **Stand Out** / Seize God-moments to make culture-shaping choices.
- **Stand Strong** / Embrace God-sized dreams to become a catalyst for change.

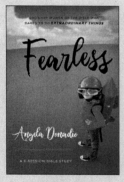

Readers will find their fearless in the inspiring stories of ordinary women of the Bible who dared to do extraordinary things.

www.angeladonadio.com

ISBN: 978-1-61036-401-0